Dog Training
with a Head Halter

Miriam Fields-Babineau

Photography by Evan Cohen

BARRON'S

Dedication

This book is dedicated to my husband, Mike, and son, Kyle. Thanks for your love, patience, and understanding.

Disclaimer

The American Society for the Prevention of Cruelty to Animals does neither encourage nor discourage the use of the particular style of head halter that is being promoted by the author of this book, Miriam Fields-Babineau.

All inquiries should be addressed to:
Barron's Educational Series, Inc.
250 Wireless Boulevard
Hauppauge, New York 11788
http://www.barronseduc.com

International Standard Book No. 0-7641-1236-8
Library of Congress Catalog Card No. 99-50239

Library of Congress Cataloging-in-Publication Data
Fields-Babineau, Miriam.
     Dog training with head healters / by Miriam Fields-Babineau ;
  photography by Evan Cohen.
     p. cm.
  ISBN 0-7641-1236-8
     1. Dogs—Training—Equipment and supplies. 2. Head halters.
  I. Title.
SF431.F543   2000
636.7'088'7—dc21   99-50239

Printed in Hong Kong
9 8 7 6 5 4 3 2 1

Table of Contents

Discussion of the history and use of head halters. Statements from
animal professionals who recommend halters and from people
who use them on their pets.

Why the head halter is more effective than other training devices.
Proper fit of the head halter. Typical first reactions to having the
head halter put on. Not a muzzle, but can control aggression.

Effective use of vocal tones and visual cues. Alpha versus Omega
position in the pack. The importance of eye contact. Consistency
and training maintenance. The basics of using food or toy reward
and targeting. Degrees of praise. The three P's of training (praise,
patience, and persistence). Equipment required for training.

Why to begin training while the dog is very young. Dealing with
a limited attention span. Make sure timing of release and reward
are perfect. Incorporating puppy kindergarten into working with
a halter. Puppy games.

Foreword

The most valuable lesson to be learned from utilizing the material in this book for educating your canine companion is that in the real world there is no such thing as an "instant Lassie." A good relationship between human and dog demands sympathy and understanding. One must be able to see things from the dog's point of view. Only through commitment, consistency, patience, and praise will your relationship with your canine pal blossom into a truly meaningful experience.

In this book, Miriam Fields-Babineau has meticulously set forth a blueprint for achieving that goal. The reader who chooses to steadfastly abide by this blueprint will discover a whole new and rewarding human/dog relationship.

Alice DeGroot, B.S., M.S., D.V.M.

Acknowledgments

First, I would like to thank Teresa Patton for showing me that head halters do work well and how to use them properly. Second, I want to thank my veterinarian, Dr. Thomas S. Eshbach, D.V.M. for all his help in locating names and phone numbers of other animal professionals who promote the use of head halters. I would also like to thank Dr. Alice DeGroot, D.V.M. for enlightening me with the proper terms and behavioral basis for using head halters. I also wish to thank Alice for her head halter invention: the K-9 Kumalong and also for writing the foreword. Dr. Alice DeGroot, D.V.M. is truly a pioneer.

I want to thank all those who wrote paragraphs about their use of head halters, Dr. Robert Anderson, D.V.M. for his advice and critique, Dr. Peter Borchelt and John Levy Jr. for making their products available. I also want to thank my photographer, Evan Cohen, for all his enthusiasm and hard work.

Chapter 1

Introduction

O f the thousands of published books about dog training and all the "different" methods—traditional, lure and reward, clicker training—there is one common denominator: a neck collar. Humans have been leading dogs by the neck for centuries. Those times are now over. Dogs can now enjoy their training and be taught humanely through the use of head halters. Head halters have proved to be not only faster but, when used properly, painless. Dogs are never choked or dragged. Now your dog will happily do what you want because **you** told him, and he easily learns to understand what you are saying.

Dogs were domesticated and accepted into our villages, farms, and homes long before horses were. Canines and humans had similar predatory attributes, making them perfect counterparts. As they domesticated horses, humans quickly learned that they lacked control when trying to lead them by their necks. After trying various methods, humans invented halters to guide horses' heads. Thereafter, most prey animals, from oxen to goats and sheep, were led with halters or pushed from behind. We also quickly learned that trying to force a prey animal into an uncomfortable situation was not only frustrating, but often unsuccessful. Most of the animals that we used for carrying or pulling far outweighed us.

From early history until the 1960s, dogs, too, were often trained using force and pain. A collar was put around their necks, and if the handler was not knowledgeable in the proper use of the collar, they were jerked into position and choked when bad. Most of the time they had no idea why they were mistreated but, being the consummate pet, and having a social hierarchy similar to our own, they complied as best they could, and eventually they learned what their masters desired. Some forgot their mistreatment. Those that rebelled were often euthanized, given away, or abandoned.

K-9 Kumalong

In 1965 Michael Fox, John Scott, John Fuller, and Clarence Pfaffenberger reported their findings on canine communication, learning processes, and behavior. The 1970s brought the British trainer, Barbara Woodhouse, into millions of homes through her books and television shows, increasing public awareness of how much dogs need to be trained. People became more cognizant of the importance of training their pets. However, the same elements remained—neck collars and choke chains.

Halti

In the late 1970s Dr. Alice DeGroot, an American veterinarian, noticed that horses and dogs could be controlled in similar ways. Through her work with rescued Irish Wolfhounds, Dr. DeGroot discovered that leading a dog by the head, as one would walk a horse, offered a less negative experience, faster learning, and better control without having to match muscle strength. The head halter worked, not only in teaching basic commands, but also in overcoming destructive behaviors. Through her behavioral studies and training skills, she invented the K-9 Kumalong, which was patented in 1984. Logical training was born. Where the head goes, the body follows.

Head halters not only reduce a dog's ability to pull, but also mimic the way mother dogs communicate with their puppies. When a youngster misbehaves, she grabs him by the muzzle and growls. The halter, when pulled down on the muzzle, is similar to mother's message. The neck strap, positioned behind the ears, maintains the position of the nose strap. Thus, the halter works in several ways: reducing the dog's pull by up to 90 percent (a real boon to a small person trying to train a large dog) and showing the dog that his handler maintains the Alpha position.

In 1984 Dr. Robert K. Anderson, D.V.M., Ruth Foster, and Jeffrey Levine developed the figure 8 head halter—the Gentle Leader. The Gentle Leader was the second type of head halter developed and patented in the United States. The Gentle Leader utilizes a similar type of pressure but is more difficult for the dog to remove. This device combines a regular collar and a halter, allowing the user to walk a well-behaved dog with a neck collar and a poorly behaved dog with the head halter. When the head halter portion is no longer required, the strap becomes a pull tab when training the dog off-lead. The pull tab

BeHave

Gentle Leader

is a means of regaining control of a dog that presents a minor challenge for the handler, such as not heeling in the proper position.

Another figure 8 halter, the BeHave, was developed by Nancy David and John Doerr of Carlsbad, California. The BeHave also offers the user the options of using it either as a regular collar, head halter, or choke collar. The BeHave also includes a leash, making it an all-in-one product.

The Gentle Leader and BeHave halters have a clip below the jaw that can tighten the nose strap, making it more difficult for the dog to remove the halter. These products were designed to allow dog owners to leave the halter on while in the house with their dog, as an aid in reducing in-home behavior problems.

Dr. Roger Mugford, Ph.D., a British psychologist, developed a head halter similar in style to Dr. DeGroot's K-9 Kumalong—the Halti. Haltis have been sold in the United States since the mid-1980s. With an adjustable neck strap and always loose nose piece, it is utilized very similarly to a horse's halter. It guides the dog's head without restriction and, as with the other head hal-

ters, can be used to control lunging and aggression.

The Snoot Loop (patent pending), developed by Dr. Peter Borchelt, Ph.D., is another conventional halter based on Dr. DeGroot's K-9 Kumalong. This head halter allows for more variation in head shape, with adjustable back, sides, and nose loop. Dr. Borchelt has also recently developed a head halter for use

Snoot Loop

Comfort Halter

on dogs with brachiocephalic (short) noses, such as Pugs, Boston Terriers, and English Bulldogs.

The latest head halter to enter the market is the Comfort Halter, designed by the author of this book. Of similar design to the K-9 Kumalong, it offers a thinner, softer nose piece, is easily adjustable, and has a neck strap that does not loosen with use.

As a dog owner, you want to be assured that your beloved pet will learn to behave and not be hurt in the process. Although it is impossible to entirely abolish all negative factors in training, eliminating as many as possible makes for more effective schooling. It is a proven fact that both dogs and people learn faster if they are not grappling with each other at the same time. Not only is the head halter the easiest means of controlling your dog, it also renders all other training devices obsolete.

Head halters are easy to use, the communication is clearer, and dogs learn faster. No more going for a walk and returning with one arm longer than the other. No more damaging a dog's neck from improper use of a choke chain. And no need to cause pain, as with a pinch collar or an electronic collar, to obtain a response. In fact, head halters work very well on dogs that are pain tolerant, dominating, and/or unresponsive to bait. Halters can be used on puppies or adult dogs of almost any temperament with positive results.

People around the world are learning about the ease and logic in training with a halter. Seminars, animal expositions, and conferences are relaying the message that there is a better way; a more humane way to train your dog. Teach your dog using logic, not pain. Use a head halter. Your dog will learn faster.

Introduction

HERE ARE A FEW COMMENTS FROM PROFESSIONALS WHO RECOMMEND HEAD HALTERS AND DOG OWNERS WHO USE THEM. (ANY MENTION OF BRAND NAMES HAVE BEEN CHANGED TO [HEAD HALTER] FOR THE PURPOSE OF REMAINING OBJECTIVE):

From unruly puppies to large, out-of-control, aggressive dogs, [head halters] are an essential tool for controlling dogs and correcting problem behaviors. Play biting and unruliness can easily be controlled, even by owners who are not as strong or as agile as their exuberant young dogs. Dogs that are aggressive to other dogs are more manageable and treatment is safer. Using a [head halter] gives owners of dominant aggressive dogs confidence and more control. When working with territorial problems, barking and growling at visitors can quickly and easily be interrupted so the owner can begin rewarding quiet behavior. For a wide variety of behavior problems and all types of dogs, using a head halter has made my job much easier. One of the best aspects about using a head halter is that it gives the owner control without the use of pain—unlike other devices that have commonly been used, such as pinch collars.

Head halters are effective, safe, humane tools for helping the veterinary staff control problem dogs. I think they are so important and helpful that they should be used in every veterinary practice. In our hospital, the [head halter] is an invaluable tool that has proven itself over and over again. It permits my staff to control unruly, fractious, frightened, and aggressive patients with a minimum of force. For example, a head halter allows the handler to restrain a fearful dog for a nail trim or other minor procedure with a minimum of duress. This makes the procedure safer and easier for the personnel and more comfortable for the pet. An aggressive dog usually does much better when the owner puts a head halter on the pet before entering the hospital. By taking immediate control, the pet is on the whole calmer, more quiet and under control. My receptionists especially appreciate this since a dog with a head halter can easily be prevented from lunging at other dogs or toward people in the waiting room.

Dr. Wayne Hunthausen, D.V.M.
Director, Animal Behavior Consultants, Westwood, KS, Past president of
the American Veterinary Society of Animal Behavior, co-author of the books,
AAHA Practioners Guide to Pet Behavior Problems and **The Handbook
of Behavior Problems of the Dog and Cat**

While not a solution for every behavioral problem, simply wearing a halter seems to have a calming effect on many excitable or anxious dogs. Used properly, they can be very useful in shaping behavior from basic obedience training to working with clinical behavior problems like dominant aggression. Halters are an excellent way to reduce pulling on walks, even by untrained dogs. How many times have we seen dogs taking their people for a walk instead of the other way around? Furthermore, halters accomplish these goals without using pain as a motivating factor or introducing fear into the human-pet relationship.

Dr. Thomas S. Eshbach, D.V.M.
Aquia-Garrisonville Animal Hospital
Stafford, VA

When we first got our dog he was a nightmare on the leash. He would pull so hard on the leash that we would be worn out after walking him. We tried choke chains and pinch collars but neither worked nearly as well as the [head halter]. Since we started using it his training sessions have been going great.

Tim & Heidi Lacky
Alexandria, VA

I have owned dogs for over thirty years, and the [head halter] has fundamentally changed the way I interact with my dogs. In the past all training was with the choke collar. For my larger, more dominant dogs, like my male Labrador Retriever, it was always a battle of wills with the choke collar. But this all changed when I had my newest dog begin training with the [head halter]. It leads her naturally without having to use brute force. I believe she is training easier and better than any of our previous dogs. In fact, I am retraining all of my dogs to the [head halter] and they are taking to it quite well. I strongly recommend the [head halter] as a superior method of training your dog.

John Ruf
Stafford, VA

Our experience with the [head halter] has been extremely positive. Before being introduced to the [head halter] our two German Shepherds (60 and 90 pounds) were impossible to walk because of their constant pulling on the leash. We finally resorted to choke collars, to no avail. Our dogs still pulled incessantly, only we were choking them in the process. Once we tried the [head halter], the difference was immediate. Our dogs stopped pulling right away, and when used in conjunction with obedience training, the [head halter] also helped us gain more control. We feel that it is a much more humane and efficient way to train dogs. We are now able finally to enjoy walks with our dogs! I even recommended the [head halter] to a friend for use with her two German Shorthairs, and the results with her dogs were equally amazing.

Andrea & Jim Jones
Stafford, VA

After trying a variety of collars on our one-year-old German Shepherd we found the [head halter] to be, by far, the best. Our Shepherd's response to the [head halter] was positive and immediate. She was far less resistant to being controlled via the [head halter], and this resulted in much less tugging and pulling on her part. Her compliance through the use of the [head halter] made training her a much easier process.

John Daly
Woodbridge, VA

I have a rescued Coonhound that would drag me around. I purchased a [head halter] and now have no problems walking him. In fact, my nine-year-old son and five-year-old daughter can walk him as well. I find halters to be a godsend. It does take some getting used to since they [dogs] are not used to things on their face, but once they do, they love them.

Leslie Thomas
Animal Rescue Foundation
Calgary, Alberta, Canada

Chapter 2

How the Head Halter Works

Why do veterinarians prescribe a head halter for their patients? Because it's a logical way to train dogs and control their bad habits. Unlike choke chains and other neck pulling devices, head halters operate on a more natural level by teaching the dog that the handler is in charge. Each time you pull or push on your pet, chemicals (endorphins) are released that provoke a physical reaction. A pull on the neck signals to the brain that one must pull back. To some dogs, pain around the neck signals that they must pull back **and** (in some individuals) be aggressive about it.

If you are walking your dog, Scruffy, down the street, and he sees another dog, he may pull at the leash to go say hello. If you pull back against him, Scruffy becomes more emphatic about his greeting, which may lead to his fur standing up along his spine, growling, and barking. If, by chance, he gets loose at this point, he might go after the other dog and fight with him instead of playing, as he'd originally intended. Sometimes the frustration can cause displaced or redirected aggression, which can result in someone getting bitten.

Inadvertently, you have made Scruffy aggressive toward other dogs. Now every time he sees one, he barks and growls. Should he have a chance to socialize, he does so aggressively, making him the neighborhood bully. Worse, if he tries to bully another dominant dog, there's bound to be a really big fight.

The head halter works in an opposite manner from the choke chain. It tells the dog that you are in charge, and he is not to react to any distraction.

When you apply this pressure over the muzzle, you are relaying the message, "Pay attention! I'm in charge." Most dogs want nothing more than to know where their place lies in their family pack. When they know there's already a leader, they relax and listen to their leader.

Now when you go for a walk and Scruffy sees that very inviting dog coming toward him, he will watch for your reaction. Should he try to say hello, all you need to do is apply the appropriate pressure. He'll stop his anxious behavior and return to watching you. There is no aggression of any kind, so when Scruffy is allowed to play with other dogs he isn't overly dominating. Best of all, you didn't have to become a weight lifter to control him.

Why, do you ask, does a little piece of nylon around the dog's head reduce your need to use muscle, whereas a heavy chain or prong collar increases that need? The answer is simple. Where a dog's head goes the rest of him will follow. You are not using muscle against muscle with a head halter. With a regular neck collar your dog can pull against it with all his weight. Along with the added leverage of four legs and being closer to the ground, he can easily drag you along behind him. A neck collar allows Scruffy to move his head in any direction he wishes and his body follows.

Collars are used on oxen, horses, or other animals that draw carts. They throw their weight behind the device and push against the pressure. Dogs do the same thing.

Until a horse is very well trained, it is always led from place to place with a halter. The halter guides the head, which in turn controls the rest of the half ton (or heavier) body. Can you imagine trying to walk a horse down the road with only a choke chain around his neck? It would more likely be the horse taking you for a walk to the nearest yard with sweet grass. How many of your neighbors would appreciate their yard work going down the tubes in a matter of minutes?

Halters are used for a very good reason. As a horse tries to get ahead of his leader, he is turned around or the halter is tugged on in order to make him slow down. Once you have control of his head, the rest of him follows. This is far easier than trying to pull back on an animal with so much weight behind it. Once the horse learns how to walk with a halter, an eleven-year-old child or one even younger can easily lead it around.

The head halter offers you more leverage and control, as well as using the key pressure point to make Scruffy pay attention. These factors together mean that he will not only learn faster but also be happier because he'll understand what you want. A dog that easily pleases his person is often more satisfied, relaxed, and likely to look forward to each training session, even if it is a simple walk around the block. Once trained off-lead, Scruffy can easily be led with a light touch on his neck collar or, better yet, with nothing but voice commands and body language.

Fitting the Head Halter

Head halters differ slightly in style, and you should follow the directions on their enclosed literature for a proper fit. Some have videos available. Be sure to view them. This is very important, for an ill-fitted, improperly used head halter can have devastating effects, as can any improperly used training device.

How will you know which size? It's easy to understand what size choke chain to get but that's not true of the halter. You can't measure around the dog's head and add two inches as you do with a choke chain. Unless using the BeHave or Snoot Loop head halters (they come in the basic sizes of small, medium, and large), you can't say, "Well, he's a medium-sized dog, so he wears a medium."

Many head halters range in sizes from 0–5, with 0 being the smallest and 5 the largest. The best way to make sure that Scruffy has the right size is to take him with you into the store and try the halter on. Begin by guessing his approximate size using the following characteristics: breed, age, and weight.

Not only do dogs come in all sizes and shapes, but they also vary within their own breeds. For example, a male dog will have a larger head than a female dog. Also, a dog with thicker fur will need a larger size than one with a thinner coat. Thus, a rough-coated dog may require a larger size than a

Make sure you can fit two fingers between the halter straps and your dog.

smooth-coated dog. (See appendix for sizing suggestions.) Please first read Chapter 5: Sit for Attention, before attempting to put the halter on your dog.

Head halters should first be fitted by placing the neck strap just behind the ears. Adjust the neck strap until the fit is snug but, you can still easily fit one or two fingers between the strap and your dog. Anything looser would allow your dog to remove the head halter easily. Next, remove the neck strap and place the nose strap over your dog's muzzle. Then click on the neck strap. The nose strap should rest a quarter inch to a full inch below the eyes (depending on the breed); the nose loop should be even with the back of his mouth, and be loose enough for your dog to open his mouth all the way. A halter that fits well will allow your dog to pant, drink, and eat.

Head halters are adjustable, so make sure the size you buy will expand for a growing dog. Many dogs change sizes even as adults. If Scruffy is still a puppy, you will need to obtain several halters to accommo-

Measure your dog's head just behind the ears.

date him as he matures. As a puppy, a small to medium breed of dog may need to start with a size 0 or small, while a larger breed can begin with a size 1. A giant-sized breed, such as a Saint Bernard, may need to begin with a size 2, which, in some brands, is a medium.

For several reasons, you should consider not using the head halter with toy breeds unless absolutely necessary, such as if the dog is an excessive barker or aggressive. First of all, unless you are the size of a Barbie doll, it will be difficult to use the downward pull to slow them while heeling. This can cause much distress to your back and legs. Not only that, toy breeds are so small they don't offer the arm-breaking pull of a larger dog. A simple turn or quick tug and release is sufficient to correct them while using a regular buckle or snap-on collar. I also highly recommend that you never use a thin choke chain on a toy breed. These dogs are very fragile, and incorrect use of a choke chain can result in tracheal and laryngeal damage.

You can use the same verbal and visual cues to train your toy dog as you would with a dog using a head halter. The communication remains the same.

Typical First Reactions

Do you recall how that new knit hat felt when you first put it on? Boy, did it itch! You scratched and pulled at it, and, if the weather wasn't too cold, you left it home. That's how dogs feel the first time they wear a head halter. Something foreign is attached to their faces, and they'll do anything to get rid of it. Even a horse that is unfamiliar with a halter will display the same behavior.

This behavior may include rubbing their faces on the ground or on solid objects, pawing at the halter, or opening their mouths wide and straining. If dogs are not shown that the halter includes a positive experience, they'll keep working at it until it's off. The best

Introducing the figure 8 halter.

Once the nose piece is in place, snap the straps behind the ears.

The head halter should not restrict mouth movement. Your dog should be able to pant, eat, drink, and play ball.

means of overcoming any initial negative reaction is to distract the dog with food or a toy.

You will find that the more dominant and challenging the dog, the longer it takes to adjust to a head halter. This occurs most frequently in adolescent dogs who have never learned any manners. Often, as soon as you begin teaching your dog to heel and sit, he forgets about the strange object on his face. Keep your dog busy and enjoying himself. After a short time, he'll have good associations and will almost put the head halter on himself.

Even when they're generally acclimated to the head halter, many dogs continue to rub it against their handler's legs when they stop moving or push their heads against the ground as they walk. Others will perform their recalls and then stick their heads between their handler's legs with the idea of getting a rub on both sides of their faces at the same time.

Yes, the halter can sometimes annoy your dog, but it is also a very humane and logical means of training him, especially if he is either not tempted by food rewards, already pulls on the leash, or exhibits a forceful personality. Halters can be useful to those dog owners who wish to train their dogs without food because they dislike the sticky pockets that result. Head halters also offer a way to work with your dog that doesn't require you to grow an additional arm to hold the leash, a toy or treat, and a noise-making device while at the same time keeping one hand free for the occasional leg slap to urge your dog forward. While proper timing of your vocal and body language is essential to any type of animal training, the fewer training devices you have to employ during the process, the easier it will be for everybody. Using a head halter, all you'll really need are your voice, body language, head halter, and leash.

If your dog is motivated by food or play, and you wish to use treats or a favorite toy in the initial training stages to increase Scruffy's positive associations and improve his response time, bait will prove beneficial. Food or a toy reward during off-lead training will also improve your dog's positioning during the heel and recall exercises. All bait can eventually be phased out over a short time so that your dog learns to listen to you and not think of you solely as a food dispenser.

People's Reactions

People often have negative reactions the first time they see a head halter. Your neighbors and friends will be curious about the device, thinking it a muzzle. "Hey, does your dog bite?" That's the most common question. Then there are the reactions from those walking their own pulling dogs: "Keep that mean dog away from me!" Meanwhile, you and Scruffy are prancing happily along, neither hurting nor disturbing anyone.

Do not be put off by these reactions. You are using a very humane training device and can declare this to those who have negative responses. Head halters are recommended by the Humane Society of the United States and the American Society for the Prevention of Cruelty to Animals. These associations would **not** advocate the use of a device that is abusive to dogs.

Be sure to tell those people who react poorly about the miracles of Scruffy's head halter. They and their dogs need enlightenment. Spread the word!

The head halter is **not** a muzzle, but can be used to control pushy and/or aggressive dogs far more easily than can any neck collar. In fact, many veterinarians, including Dr. Wayne Hunthausen, D.V.M., director, Animal Behavior Consultants, Westwood, KS, past president of the American Veterinary Society of Animal Behavior, co-author of the books, **AAHA Practioners Guide to Pet Behavior Problems** and **The Handbook of Behavior Problems of the Dog and Cat,** are now using head halters on nervous dogs while doing examinations or inoculations. Wearing the head halter, the dogs calm down and veterinary technicians can better control them without the fear of being bitten. (Methods of controlling aggression will be discussed in a later chapter.) The head halter will give you more control, properly correct the dog without undue pain, and safely prevent any future outbursts, all without hitting, yelling, or using muscle.

Head halters teach, cure, and prevent, because you are in control, using techniques your dog understands quickly.

Chapter 3

Can We Talk?

All dogs need jobs. They have been specifically bred to perform a particular task, be it herding, hunting, guarding, or pulling. Training sessions offer your dog a positive, constructive means of channeling his energy and desire to perform a job. Obedience training not only satisfies these instincts, it also brings you closer to your dog than you ever thought possible. Can you imagine talking to your dog and not only having him understand you, but being able to understand him?

Before you begin any training, you need to learn how to speak canine. Dogs communicate through visual cues and verbal tones. Taste, touch, and odor also play large roles, but because **we** need to convey the message, we'll concentrate on **our** strong points, which are verbal and visual skills.

We will need to keep our communication as basic as possible. Dogs don't understand long explanations or mixed messages. To them the world is black and white. Cut

and dry. All or none. Canines don't know about gray areas. Thus, when you show dislike of a behavior only when it inconveniences you, your dog becomes frustrated. They don't understand "maybe," "sometimes," and "you can do it this time but not next time." They don't realize when you're wearing nice clothes or casual clothes. They don't understand why guests can't be as fun as their own people. Dogs also don't comprehend our age groups very well. Yes, they know how much fun children are (racing after and jumping around yipping and erratically moving people is lots of fun), but often they don't understand that they must be gentle with the elderly or physically challenged.

Almost everyone can learn to use their voice and body language in the canine style. It is as simple as using three different tones of voice and two distinct body positions. Best of all, you needn't have any special training equipment to make use of your talents. You'll always have your voice (unless you have laryngitis), and there are always ways to use body motions. Once your dog is trained, you can put away all training devices because you'll be able to communicate completely through your voice and body.

Vocal Tones

There are three tones of voice to use when training: the praise tone, the command tone, and the reprimand tone. The praise tone should be an enthusiastic high and happy tone of voice. Pair the praise tone with the word "good." Learning a simple word is far easier for the dog than phrases. Remember how babies learn our language. They don't begin by speaking sentences. They begin with single words, then eventually group them together in twos and threes. As with human communication, dogs first learn our language in single word usage. Eventually, they learn phrases and sentences. Dr. DeGroot states that dogs can easily learn more than 200 words and phrases by the time they are a year old, or even more, should you care to put the time into teaching them.

Use the command tone of voice with authority. Always precede a command with your dog's name. His name should never be used with a low reprimanding tone, nor should you use it solely **as** a reprimand. His name should always have positive associations. Give all commands only one time. This way Scruffy learns to respond on the first and only command, not after ten or twelve when he tires of your babble and accidentally does what you asked. Each command should be as follows: "Scruffy, sit." "Scruffy, heel." "Scruffy, stay." Be sure to speak clearly and

never, ever shout. Dogs hear at **least** twice as well as we do. Your dog will hear your lightest whisper. So don't yell—**demand.** You are telling him to do it, not asking him. You can use a pleasant command tone for such things as heel and recall and use a more adamant tone for sit, stay, and, especially, the down command. An adamant voice is not a shout or mean tone of voice, just a demanding attitude.

When reprimanding, use a low, growly tone of voice. You want to sound like an aggressive dog when you reprimand. Any dog will understand this tone. The word that you use with your aggressive, low tone doesn't matter. You can use the word "No!" or, if you're opposed to saying no, you can use "Anh!" Think of how your mother sounded when she would catch you about to do something wrong. She'd say, "Anh, anh, anh, don't do that!" You can also use the word "Bad!" Whatever you use, be sure to use the same word every time and always say it in a low, growly tone of voice. To simplify matters, I'll use the word "No!" in this book. Just remember you can use any word with your tones; simply be consistent in the usage and don't offer a long explanation. Scruffy won't catch a word of it.

You'll need to practice changing from the high tones of reward to the low tones of reprimand and back. It's the tones of voice that your dog is responding to. Learning the meanings of your words comes later. You must first speak canine before Scruffy can learn human speech.

Body Language

Body language is very useful when training your dog. Two main body positions will aid your overall communication. The first is the upright position. Remain upright whenever you give a command or reprimand. Scruffy won't respect your word as much if you're at eye level, for you are in an "equal" position, not that of a dominant pack member.

The second position is to crouch down to Scruffy's level. This is called the submissive or equal position. Use this when you greet, play, or release Scruffy from work. Crouching down will offer your dog the opportunity to greet you properly instead of having to jump up to do so. Be careful, however, if Scruffy is a large dog. You can get bowled over. Case in point: Scruffy is playing in the yard and you want to say hello. You crouch down and open your arms, telling him to come. Scruffy sees the equivalent of bowling pins at the end of a lane. On he comes, full speed ahead and then, strike! He scores, knocking you over and instantly slobbering your face with wet kisses. Should Scruffy be large, you may want to bend at the waist and knees instead of going all the way down.

Crouching or bending at the waist when releasing Scruffy from work helps tell him that it's time to rest. It's important to communicate the differences between work and play time.

All dogs need frequent breaks during training sessions. This increases their learning capacity and enjoyment. It is helpful to use a word associated with the release times. Whatever you use, make sure it isn't something that you often use in conversation, or while training. The word "Break" is good because you rarely use that word at any other time.

The worst word you could use is "Okay" to release your dog from work because you often use it in normal conversation. In my many years of training people to work with their dogs, I have heard, "Okay, Heel,"

numerous times. Apparently there are a lot of dogs out there named "Okay." If you want to name your dog that, this is fine. Just don't use the same word to release him. It's confusing for your dog to be released as he's getting a command.

Another important precedent to establish at the beginning of training is that **you** are the boss. This matters a great deal because the dog pack has a clear hierarchy. The Alpha dog (or top dog) gets everything first, including preferential feeding, bedding, and breeding privileges. Should Scruffy believe that he is the Alpha dog in your family, he could become dominating, nervous, and destructive. He can also become possessive and territorially aggressive—very dangerous behaviors. Each time someone tries to move him or take something away, they risk being growled at or bitten.

Most dogs are very agreeable to being lower in the pecking order. In fact, they thrive on it because they no longer have all the leadership responsibilities. It's tough having to make sure everyone behaves, and those territory patrols can become tiresome. Teaching your dog his place goes hand in hand with proper obedience training. This is how you are teaching Scruffy to listen to you no matter what is going on around you and to respond immediately—not when he chooses. With behavior modification, Scruffy will learn what is and is not acceptable. He'll learn the rules of the house and will become a happy, well-mannered companion (see Chapter 17 for behavior modification techniques).

Accomplishing any goal requires one key ingredient: consistency. This is the only way you can make sure Scruffy both understands and responds to everything you say. Once your dog is trained, you can consistently associate any particular word or phrase with an action, and he'll pick up on the meaning in a short time. Remaining consistent is easier than you think. Simply give and follow through your commands regardless of the situation. For example, Scruffy is heeling nicely in your back yard, but then doesn't behave as well when he's walking around the block and sees other dogs, children, bicycles, and balls rolling past him. They are so tantalizing that he begins pulling on his leash. The worst thing you can do is change the way you handle the situation. Continue to work him exactly as you did in the back yard. Consistency teaches Scruffy to be a good citizen wherever he goes.

One of the main canine capers of maintaining the Alpha position is eye contact. Should Scruffy not respond to your command, you can often use direct eye contact to reinforce what you said without having to actually place your dog into position. For example, you told Scruffy to sit. He stands and ignores your command. You look directly in his eyes with a stern expression. Most likely Scruffy will look away and place his little bottom down. In this manner you have corrected him without having to say a single word and without any physical reprimand.

Close up of dog targeting.

However, you **did** reprimand. You did a canine reprimand.

Another important aspect of ensuring that Scruffy turns out to be the most wonderful dog in the world is to maintain his training. During the initial training he must be worked daily. This constant reinforcement will deeply embed the behaviors. Once Scruffy has finished his training and becomes reliable in all situations, you can decrease the number of lessons. However, Scruffy will not like this and may rebel by doing something bad to get your attention. For example, Scruffy has been in training for six months when your schedule suddenly becomes so full that you don't have time to work with him. Perhaps it's been about a week since your last training session. One day you come home and find a big hole in the living room carpet and Scruffy sulking in the corner. He did this to get the attention that he'd been receiving. Yes, he'd rather get positive attention, but any attention is better than none.

Targeting

Before starting any training you will need to obtain Scruffy's attention. Not only that, but with the added distraction of the head halter, you'll need to use a very inviting means of doing so. The best approach to getting any dog's attention is through the use of food or a favorite toy. Before you even put on the head halter, figure out which type of treat or toy will get most of Scruffy's attention. Some dogs will go crazy over a tennis ball, while others will drop their toy in preference of freeze-dried liver or piece of hot dog.

Once you have Scruffy's attention, you can begin teaching him to target. This exercise will build on his attention by having him learn to place his nose near the reward. Targeting involves the use of operant conditioning. In a nutshell, operant conditioning consists of teaching the subject to perform a specific behavior and, eventually, chain of behaviors to receive his reward. Most animal training is based on this concept.

Begin by holding the reward in your hand. Once Scruffy puts his nose on your hand, praise him by saying, "Good boy!" in a happy tone of voice while simultaneously giving him the reward. Do this several times. Scruffy will learn this concept very quickly. Nose to hand means reward.

After three or four repetitions, move your hand slowly from side to side. As Scruffy watches his target moving, praise him. Now you are using the praise to bridge the space between the action and his receiving the reward. Scruffy hears the praise and knows that his reward is soon to follow. At the beginning, do not move your hand more than a few times before giving him his reward. As you progress, increase the motion. Move your hand up and down as well as side to side. Scruffy's nose should follow your hand the entire way as you praise him.

Now you have established the means of obtaining and rewarding Scruffy's attention. Not only that, you've learned how to speak canine using your voice and body language. You now know how to use operant conditioning to achieve results.

P's and Q's

Remember the old saying, "Mind your P's and Q's"? The world of dog training has a variation: Maintain the three P's of training—patience, persistence, and praise. It takes all three to become a successful dog trainer.

Patience is indeed a virtue. You must remain calm and relaxed throughout the process. No matter how much Scruffy tries to go his own way, you must continue to work on gaining his attention in a way he understands. Losing your patience teaches Scruffy that you have a breaking point. Once you reach it, he can have his own way. This makes a dog more difficult to control and teaches him that he's got the upper paw. Never give in. Scruffy will learn good behavior much more rapidly.

Persistence will overcome all obstacles. No matter how many times Scruffy tries to say hello to another dog while you are walking, you must make him behave and remain attentive to you. Should you be working with a dog between the ages of five months and a year and a half, this can be very trying. However, persevere, and within a short time Scruffy will shed his allegiance to you.

Praise is of the utmost importance throughout the training process. Never skimp on praise. Scruffy adores your praise and will do anything to receive it. Once you have dispensed with the treats and the leash, praise is all you have to reinforce your dog's good deeds. During the training process you will have several degrees of praise available. The better Scruffy's response, the better the reward. For example, you are trying to teach Scruffy to sit properly at your side, facing forward. Currently, he is having to be placed in the Sit and is sitting crookedly. You begin by praising him and giving a treat when you place him. Next, while you still praise him when you must place him in the Sit, you only give the treat when he sits on his own. As he becomes adept at sitting on command, you begin requiring him to sit closer to you before receiving the treat. Always continue to praise him when he sits, but he only gets the treat if he sits properly. Also, you can control the

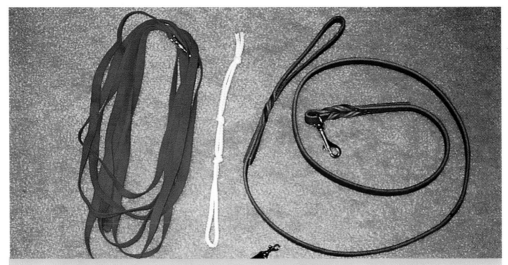

Training equipment: The six-foot leather leash for on-lead training.
The twenty-foot cotton leash for long-distance work.

exuberance of your voice to fit the occasion. A Sit on command off to the side warrants a "Good boy," while a closer Sit warrants a **"Good boy!"** and a pat on the head. A perfect Sit warrants a **"Good boy!!!"** with a treat and lots of petting. Scruffy will quickly figure out that the **best** things come to dogs who perform perfectly. These variable degrees of praise can be used to improve **any** behavior in a fun and humane manner.

Equipment Required for Training

As you've probably figured out by now, you'll definitely need a head halter for the training process. Before each training session you will need to check the halter's adjustment because they often work themselves loose with use, and the material stretches.

I highly recommend using a four-to-six foot leash while training. Should Scruffy be an easily distracted and large breed of dog, you may want to use a leather leash. You can use any type of leash with a medium or small dog. Regardless of the type of leash, make sure it is comfortable and hold it loosely.

There are several reasons for using a loose versus tight leash. First, you don't want to be dragging your dog from place to place. The tighter your leash, the more Scruffy will be fighting with you. Scruffy must have freedom of head movement and be allowed to make the choice to listen and learn. Second, keeping your dog's head in the uncomfortable position of always looking up or to the side can cause an upper cervical subluxation

This illustrates the proper fit of a conventional head halter.

Should you be unable to find a brace connector, you can simply attach a regular leash to Scruffy's neck collar and tie it to your belt. This works as insurance against the possibility of Scruffy shrugging out of the head halter and getting loose. The shape of some dog's heads, such as Schipperkes and Dobermans, with their small ears and/or not much difference between their neck and head sizes, means a head halter can easily be dislodged. The connector is a simple precaution, more to give you a sense of security than to make sure you don't lose your dog.

The BeHave and Gentle Leader head halters offer an alternative to a brace connector or extra leash because they are also designed to work as a regular collar should your dog push off his nose piece. While you don't want to choke or pull on your dog, losing him is worse. The BeHave and Gentle Leader designs give you a chance to reconstruct the head halter while still keeping hold of your dog.

At the beginning of training, should you use treats or a toy, I suggest a waist pouch for holding these items. You will need to keep your hands free to use the leash properly and engage in body communications. The ideal pouch will allow you easy access to the reward without having to make your dog wait, which could disrupt your timing.

Should your dog not respond to any bait, use lots of praise and petting in a favorite place. Bait is not an absolute necessity when working with a head halter, only an easier means of obtaining Scruffy's attention.

(spinal misalignment), requiring chiropractic correction.

The leash is attached to the ring on the head halter that lies below Scruffy's chin. If using a Halti, I also recommend using a lightweight connector to attach the head halter to Scruffy's regular buckle or snap-on neck collar. A lightweight brace connector, normally used to attach two dogs together while using one lead, would work well. With a clip at each end, it is ideal for attaching a head halter to the neck collar and long enough to not interfere with the training process.

Chapter 4

But, But
I'm Just a Pup!

Before you can comprehend the importance of beginning Scruffy's training while he's very young, you need to understand a few things about canine development.

First of all, puppies are born knowing how to train their people. The canine hierarchical social structure is an innate characteristic: that is, dogs are born with it or are naturally quick to learn it.

A dog is born with the capacity to be dominant or submissive and with instincts that tell him how to behave with other dogs.

Mother dog helps them develop much of this while they're still nursing, but the instinct emerges even more during the weaning and peer socialization processes between five and twelve weeks.

Puppy Behavior

A dogs' behavior matures greatly during the first year of their lives. Some canine behaviorists say dogs mature fifteen human years during their first year, while other scientists believe that they go through twenty-one years of behavioral development during their first human year. Either way, all new behaviors should be taught while a dog is young because it is at this time that their brains are like sponges, soaking up information.

Each thing you do is being filed away in Scruffy's young brain, including such behavior as "Mommy lets me cuddle with her on the couch," or "If I jump on Mommy's lap I'll get a treat." Everything you do is setting a precedent for future behaviors. For example, since you have allowed Scruffy on the couch as a puppy, he'll believe he has every right to do so as an adult, muddy paws or not. Not only that, but those cushions make great chew toys while one is playing a couch potato.

Let's say Scruffy matures by fifteen dog years during his first human year. Would you wait to teach anything to your human child until he's reached ten or fifteen years of age? This includes teaching them how to speak and behave as well as making sure they receive an academic education. Not at all! Most children learn best while young; they **enjoy** learning new things at this age. Teaching a second language, for example, is easiest while a child is in elementary school. Once in high school, their raging hormones may make it harder for them to concentrate on learning.

This also pertains to dogs. They fit well into our homes and lives because their social skills and abilities to learn are similar to our own, only greatly condensed in time. Teaching Scruffy how to behave and learn should begin while he is only two months old. Why? Because his aptitude for learning is very high. By the age of three months, he's even more open to learning. His motor skills and ability to understand are fully developed. At five months his hormones start kicking in, and he begins to resist authority. Depending on the individual and breed, this can even happen as young as four months. Why wait until Scruffy reaches the age of adolescent rebellion? Not only that, by then he has already learned that he can control you and his environment.

Starting the training process at the tender age of two months requires different techniques and short training sessions, but Scruffy will learn faster and be more eager to perform. Also, he'll know what it means to be well mannered, making his adolescence far easier for you to handle. By the age of six months, he'll already know that he cannot chew the furniture or carpets and that you are the authority figure. Why wait until the carpet has holes, you need new furnishings, and Scruffy is demanding that you play with him when you come home from work exhausted? Early learning is of the utmost importance for proper development and a good relationship.

Dogs undergo personality changes as they grow for many reasons. Besides hormonal changes, they go through bodily changes. Teething is a big part of their behavioral changes. This alone causes many different problems, such as chewing, anxiety, and overall destructive tendencies.

Teaching Scruffy to not touch table legs when he first puts his teeth on them at the tender age of two or three months will preserve your furniture from tooth marks as long as you own it. It also teaches him what is and is not a chew toy. Providing him with a variety of chew toys also helps him understand. While he's teething in earnest he'll appreciate ice cubes. These are not only lots of fun, but help numb his gums. Another way to help relieve those aching gums is to wet an old washcloth, roll it up, and freeze it. Take it out and offer him the washcloth. He'll have a great time, and you'll get a break. At last, some time to get things done.

Another great way to make sure Scruffy keeps his attention on his toys instead of on your cabinets is to offer food-filled hollow toys. Dr. Ian Dunbar, author of **Sirius Puppy Training** (book and video), suggests putting a pup's regular food inside toys, such as Buster Cubes, shank bones, and Kongs. This way Scruffy will be so into his toys that he won't even think of going after anything that isn't as tasty and rewarding.

Puppy Training

Many trainers and other animal professionals recommend holding off on formal obedience training until a dog is five or six months. They recommend this because of a puppy's short attention span. Unless this has been recommended because of a group teaching environment, and the instructor wants to make certain the dogs have received all their vaccinations, this is not a good idea. Besides, most dogs have completed their vaccination schedule by the time they are four months of age. By this time Scruffy has developed bad habits that need to be cured. Training him at the age of two months prevents him from picking up the bad habits and insures a better understanding between the two of you. Would you wait to housetrain Scruffy until he's six months old? No. You'd want it done as soon as possible. If an eight-week-old puppy can easily learn the appropriate place to relieve himself, he can also learn basic commands.

A two- to three-month-old puppy can learn any of the commands normally taught to an older puppy or adult dog. He can heel, sit, stay, lay down, and come. He can learn to listen with his toys flying through the air and behave on walks. I do recommend, however, that all initial learning is done in a distraction-free, enclosed area. I also suggest that the entire family become involved, not only to maintain consistency, but also to be sure that Scruffy learns to listen to everyone. Dogs only listen to those who work with them.

Although young puppies do have short attention spans, they can learn a lot by working in short, frequent sessions. Five or ten minutes, a couple times a day is more effective than a twenty- or thirty-minute stretch.

The short training sessions will be fun, and Scruffy will look forward to them.

To increase Scruffy's attention span, food rewards can be used. Doing a short training session before feeding time or while Scruffy has lots of energy is most productive. Puppies have great amounts of energy first thing in the morning and early in the evening. Not only will training at these times channel Scruffy's energy, but will also permit longer training sessions, which in turn will increase his attention span and work tolerance. Even if you begin training when your dog is six months, you will need to begin with short sessions. Dogs don't automatically have longer attention spans because they are older.

Puppies are easily distracted so you will need to properly time your praise, as well as reward and commands. As soon as Scruffy does what you ask, give him his treat and continue on to the next command. If you wait between giving him the reward and telling him what to do next, you will lose his attention. For example, you tell him to sit, give him the treat, and then wait a few seconds (most probably as you are searching for and breaking apart another treat) while he eats. Next thing you know he's up wandering around instead of sitting at your side. It helps to use a treat that he can eat quickly, such as freeze-dried liver, string cheese, or a small piece of jerky. Make sure it is **very** small. (Prepare them ahead of time.) This gives Scruffy the taste of a treat, but doesn't require time to chew it. Also, the use of a few **small** treats won't interfere with his normal eating patterns.

While training a puppy, or any dog, for that matter, you also need to perfectly time his release from work. You only offer release (break time) when he is performing well. Never end on a bad note. This way, Scruffy won't misinterpret your frustration for his doing something properly. The release times should occur often, given after varying exercises and combined with lots of petting and praise. This encourages Scruffy to perform.

Before starting any training, let Scruffy become used to the head halter. Let him wear it while he plays, eats, and sleeps. Never leave it on, however, if you are not in the same room watching him closely.

Initially, we are only **acclimating** Junior to the head halter, not actually using it until he has a good idea of how to perform some basic commands.

Before any training session, make sure Scruffy has had lots of rest and quiet time. Also, don't feed him at least two hours before the session; this can make him sleepy and reduce his food drive. The two of you should be in a quiet, fenced-in area without any other animals. Pick up all of Scruffy's toys before you begin. He's not yet ready for distraction-proofing.

Using bait, lure your pup's head into the head halter.

All training will begin by first attaching your training leash to Scruffy Junior's regular neck collar, so that he becomes used to having it on. Allow your pup to drag the leash around while he plays with you. Should he enjoy playing fetch, go ahead and play. Scruffy needs to learn that the leash itself will not cause him any harm and, as with all training equipment, has positive associations.

Most formal obedience training is begun with the Heel and Sit exercises, but I recommend starting puppies with the Come and Sit, then the Down, followed by the Heel, and finally the Stay. The Stay tends to be the most difficult behavior for a young puppy; they rarely sit still for very long, especially when distracted.

Puppy Kindergarten

Training puppies consists of turning the sessions into fun and games. This means that you cannot stick to formal schedules and procedures. Scruffy Junior must be having a great time and learning new behaviors simultaneously.

Because puppies are blank books and not yet filled with mischief, all training can be done in a traditional manner through the use of bait training. The main difference between the traditional puppy training and utilizing the techniques in this book are that Scruffy Junior will be wearing his head halter while working.

Head halters are a means of gaining control over a dog who has none. Most young puppies do not become willful until they reach at least four months of age. Should this not be the case with yours, and he is already pulling on the leash, then go directly to using the head halter, so that you can back up all your commands.

Puppy Kindergarten

Puppy Kindergarten is based on the Round Robin game. This game consists of two or more people standing a few feet apart. The puppy goes from one person to the next in turn. As the puppy learns how to play the game, the handlers gradually increase their distance from each other.

Round Robin begins with the Come and Sit exercise as follows:

1. Begin with targeting.
2. Scoot back a few steps as you say, "Scruffy, Come." Keep your hand near his face until he begins coming toward you. As he does, draw your hand toward your knees and stop. Be sure to offer lots of enthusiastic praise as Scruffy Junior responds.
3. When Scruffy Junior arrives, give him the treat.

This is repeated by the next person working in your circle.

As Scruffy Junior readily responds to the Come command from everyone in the circle, begin teaching him to sit when he arrives.

1. When Scruffy arrives in front of you, hold the treat just a little above his head, aiming for between his eyes. You'll want to keep it near enough to his nose for him to smell it.
2. Scruffy will look up at the treat. As he does so, say, "Scruffy, Sit." He'll most likely do this automatically because when he looks up, his rear end goes down. Should he not sit, tuck his tail under his bottom and apply pressure to the backs of his hind legs with your other hand.
3. As soon as Scruffy sits, praise him and give him his treat.
4. Each person in the circle makes Scruffy come and sit in turn.

Practice the Round Robin games both inside and outside your home. Scruffy Junior needs to learn to listen wherever you and he may be. Once he is very good at coming on command, try hiding behind a wall or door. This prepares him for listening when you are out of his line of vision.

When working with a young puppy, teach all of the behaviors through the use of the Round Robin game. For example, when teaching Scruffy to lay down or stay, you can simply incorporate it into the game by making him perform the behaviors when he arrives and sits before you.

When Scruffy has a good understanding of these exercises, you can begin doing them using the head halter. Attach the leash to the ring under his chin, using the same rewards and many breaks. At this time, too, you can begin the more formal work of teaching your puppy to heel during his training sessions.

For the most part, whether working with a puppy or an adult dog, the methods of teaching him with the use of a head halter are virtually identical.

As your puppy targets on your hand, go backward as you say, "Scruffy, Come."

Chapter 5

Sit for Attention

How can we begin to put on a head halter if Scruffy won't sit still? He keeps jumping up and moving his head from side to side, making it impossible. The only way seems to be to tackle him and force it on when he can't move. Wrong! Never force your dog to do anything. Everything needs to be positive and upbeat. If Scruffy is to look forward to working for you, you must begin by making it fun for him.

Remember the targeting exercise? You put food in your hand and Scruffy puts his nose on your hand sniffing and trying to get the food? Once he knew food was in there, he would follow your hand anywhere—up, down, left side, right side. Talk about an immediate attention grabber! Very few dogs will pass up freeze-dried liver, a piece of hot dog, or slice of cheese. There's a treat for every taste and, for some dogs, there's a toy that's even more appealing. The trick is to first discover what drives your dog. It must be something absolutely irresistible. Once he

works well for his reward, you can begin teaching him to work well for praise. Most dogs love praise more than anything else. Approval from their people is very important.

Let's begin by reviewing basic targeting. Place the bait in your hand and allow Scruffy to sniff at it. When he does, offer him the treat. Do this again, only make Scruffy turn his head to retrieve the treat. Next time, make his head go down a bit. Now make his head go up a bit. Try making his head go up a little higher. Hold the treat near enough for Scruffy to keep his nose close to your hand but not so far that he feels the need to jump up for it. What just happened? He sat! Be sure to praise him and give the treat immediately. Repeat this exercise a few times.

Once Scruffy will sit as soon as you put your targeting hand up over his nose, add the command, "Sit." Say his name first to get his attention, then say sit in a commanding tone of voice—"Scruffy, Sit." This does not mean to yell or sound abusive. Be pleasant,

Left: Using a toy helps make the introduction more pleasant. Middle: Once the dog is targeting on the bait, slide the halter over his nose. Right: As the dog eats his food or puts his mouth on a toy, snap the straps behind his ears.

but don't ask him and don't repeat the command. In other words, keep your tone level. Do not allow it to lift an octave or two as you give the command. When Scruffy's rear end touches the ground, praise and offer the treat. Remember that timing is everything. You must offer the treat quickly so that Scruffy identifies the reward with his action.

Should you have a dog who does not care about food or a toy, you will need to place him into the sit

Always obtain your dog's attention prior to beginning work.

position. The training procedures for doing so are as follows:

1. Put one hand under his chin and the other just in front of his hip bones.
2. Say, "Scruffy, Sit," as you simultaneously lift his chin and press on the hollow in front of the hip bones.
3. As soon as his bottom touches the ground, release the pressure and praise him.
4. Repeat this exercise up to ten times before trying to put on the head halter.

Be sure that Scruffy has a chance to sniff the head halter to be certain he doesn't think it's a nasty snake about to engulf him forever. Offer him a treat or toy as he sniffs the head halter. This will add the message of "nice head halter, good things happen with this head halter." Even if Scruffy is not into bait, allow him to inspect the head halter.

Begin the process by palming a treat in your hand and slipping your hand through the nose piece of the head halter. Make sure the nose piece is open wide enough to allow Scruffy to comfortably stick his nose through.

Place your hand near Scruffy and hold it above his nose, positioned between his eyes. Give him the Sit command. Wow, the perfect position to put on the head halter! His nose is up and rear end down, plus we have his attention.

Slide the nose band over Scruffy's muzzle, as you give him the treat. As he eats, quickly snap the head strap together behind his ears. If he gets up at any time, repeat the Sit exercise. You want to teach him to place his own head inside the head halter, or, at the very least, sit quietly as you put it on. You should never have to force the apparatus onto him. This only serves to teach him avoidance behavior—every time he sees the head halter he'll run.

When teaching Scruffy to sit while you are heeling with him (you will learn how to heel in the next chapter), begin with the same techniques. However, you want Scruffy to sit at your side, facing the same direction you face. To do this you'll need to keep your left hand (treat in the palm) even with and close to your left leg. Scruffy will be where the treat is. If your hand is in front of you, you are teaching him to forge ahead. If your hand is way out to the side, you are teaching him to remain away from you. For Scruffy to learn how to remain in heel position, you **must** keep your left hand **on** your left leg.

Even though you are not yet working on the Heel exercise, you can practice the Sit in Heel position by placing yourself on Scruffy's right side as you tell him to sit. This prepares him for things to come.

As you stop walking, or if you simply placed yourself in position, lift the treat over his head and slightly back, over the top of his head toward his ears. He will look up, strain-

ing his head back. As soon as he sits be sure to praise and give him his reward.

Many dogs are simply too obstinate or distracted to pay any attention at all to the treat in your hand. Either they are very well fed and another bit of food is meaningless, or the other dog they see chasing a ball is far more interesting. With their minds too busy to target, you will need to use another means of teaching the sit command.

As always, we need to begin every session by putting on the head halter. If your dog is not sitting because of nearby distractions, take him somewhere quiet and work there. If he is not targeting because he is not hungry, wait until mealtime to put on the head halter. Make sure his nose goes through the nosepiece before burying itself in the food bowl.

Now that the head halter is on, we can begin with the Sit command. When Scruffy finishes dinner allow him a few minutes to gather his wits (get all the food off his nose) and then begin.

Correction for not sitting on command. A forward and upward pull.

Sit for Attention

1. Put the leash on the little ring under Scruffy's chin.
2. Say his name and the command, Sit, pull forward and upward under his chin, as you apply gentle pressure on his rump, just in front of his hips.
3. As soon as he sits, **immediately** release the pressure and praise him.
4. Repeat the Sit exercise at least five times before releasing Scruffy from his training session.

If Scruffy does not care about the food reward, try petting him in his favorite places. Scratching the back can be heavenly. If Scruffy is a dominant dog, you should begin his rub at the top of his head and move in a firm motion down to his shoulders. This is the canine way of putting a paw over his back and saying, "I'm the boss."

Try to do training sessions in short periods of time—approximately five to ten minutes—several times throughout the day.

This dog is learning to perform a Sit/Stay at a door instead of racing through.

Practice both indoors and out. If you have other pets, don't limit the training times to when Scruffy's "siblings" are not around. Be realistic. The others will always be there, so make sure Scruffy listens in their presence.

Now that Scruffy has an idea of how to sit we can use this exercise in many different ways. The most logical is to teach him to sit at doors, gates, and whenever he desires attention. Granted, we never, ever give attention when Scruffy demands it, but we do offer it when he behaves. When he sits and looks at you, that is a good time to praise and rub. Then again, make sure he's not telling you, "I need to go outside, NOW!" Through time and observation you'll learn the difference between Scruffy's needing to go potty and his desiring attention.

Teaching him these patterns is simply a matter of persistence and consistency. Every time you answer the door, make sure you have control. Scruffy should be wearing his head halter with the "indoor" leash (any old leash that is around four feet long) attached, allowing you quick access. Before opening the door tell him to Sit. When he does, praise him, then open the door. Every time he gets up, pull forward and up on the halter. Yes, this does get tiring, especially if you **really** want to speak to that door-to-door salesman. However, if you give in and allow Scruffy to get up, he will learn to keep trying your patience until you give in and allow him to jump on your elderly mother. Also, you have just taught him how long it takes before he gets his own way. Now that's a fun doggy game! At least, it is for Scruffy, not for your elderly mother.

Keep in mind the three P's of training: patience, persistence, and praise. These apply to every situation. When Scruffy learns that you will never give in, that he must listen every time, and that he will be rewarded for doing so, he will eagerly comply.

Chapter 6

Walk with Me

Everyone longs for the time when their dog will walk at their side without pulling them down the road. We can more easily enjoy the scenery when we can look around instead of watching to make sure Scruffy is in his place at our side. With head halter training you will rarely have to look to be assured that your dog is there. In fact, it's far more important to pay attention to where you're going than to make sure Scruffy is where he should be. Scruffy will never learn to trust you as his leader if you are constantly tripping over roots and going face first into telephone poles. He'll **know** for a fact that he must take charge.

You will learn to feel on the leash whether or not Scruffy is with you. When you feel the slightest amount of tension, it's time to turn or tug down and release. When the leash is relaxed, it's time to praise. You will also feel when the leash is moving to the right or left. Always tug down and in the direction opposite the one you feel your dog pulling.

Turns will be of the utmost importance. The more turns you do the more attentive your dog will be. All turns should be 180 or 90 degrees. They should be sharp and quick.

Another thing that will be extremely helpful while training is to walk briskly. Maintaining a fast pace gives Scruffy fewer opportunities to become distracted. Walking slowly gives him the chance to sniff, which takes his attention from you. When you slow down and wait for Scruffy, he, too, slows down, causing him to lag and be unresponsive. Even looking over your shoulder at him while you walk will disrupt his cadence. He is following the movement of the left line of your body, in particular, your left shoulder. When your shoulder moves backward, he will slow down. Keeping your shoulders squared or your left shoulder a bit forward, especially when turning right, will help Scruffy maintain a proper Heel position. If you must watch your dog, and most of us do during the initial training phases, or if you are working with a toy breed, watch from the corner of your left eye, not with both eyes.

You can never overpraise your dog. Scruffy should hear "Good boy," from the time he begins a proper response until you tell him "Break." You need to guide him with your voice. He's hearing "Good" while he's performing correctly, but as soon as he isn't, he hears "No!" When he returns to the proper response he hears "Good" again. The more you speak to him, the more attentive he'll be. That doesn't mean a long conversation about the weather or who won last night's football game. He doesn't understand all those words. Keep your communication simple and differentiate your vocal tones. In other words, try not to make your reprimand sound like a command.

Starting the heeling exercise with any dog is done with bait, lots of patience, and appropriate timing. The main difference is that you will be using the leash and head halter instead of a neck collar.

First, you need to know how to hold the leash. There will be two different ways. One for when you are baiting and the other when you are simply rewarding and no longer baiting. While baiting, you need to hold the bait in your left hand. Therefore, the entire leash must be held in your right hand. You must leave the leash loose enough so that you aren't constantly pulling on Scruffy, yet tight enough so that he isn't always stepping over it. A good rule of thumb is to form a "J" between you and your dog, with your hand the uppermost part of the letter and the end of the curve attached

Before beginning to Heel, obtain your dog's attention through targeting.

How to hold the leash when using bait.

to Scruffy's head halter ring. When holding the leash with your right hand, give Scruffy about two to three feet of that leash. A tight leash means constant pulling, and a dog cannot learn if he's being dragged every which way.

Place your right thumb through the handle and gather a few loops in your right hand. Hold your right hand at your waist or lower. Never hold your arms in the air. Not only is this not the way you normally walk, but you'll tend to pull on your dog, making him struggle against you.

Everything you do is setting a precedent for the future. Unless you want Scruffy to think he can only heel when your arm is stuck up in the air, keep your arms down. Dogs associate every body movement with your commands. Therefore, try to remain upright, arms down, and step forward purposefully. You have a destination in mind, even if it's only five steps away.

Be sure you operate the head halter properly. One of the main differences when using a head halter versus a regular collar is that when you perform a correction while heeling, you tug downward and then in the direction opposite of where Scruffy is heading, instead of up, back, or to the side, as with a neck collar.

Constantly pulling Scruffy's head around to the side when he forges ahead of you does not teach him to heel because your dog is not allowed to make the choice to learn. He is being pulled on and restrained instead of given a chance to perform correctly. Dogs must be given the chance to decide whether or not to listen. If all new behaviors are taught in an understandable manner, they will usually choose to listen. However, all dogs have times when they will challenge their people, and they must be

allowed to do so to increase their knowledge of cause and effect.

Let's say Scruffy is moving off to your left instead of staying with you. You will tug down and to the right. If Scruffy is moving ahead, you tug down and back. However, should Scruffy move behind you and to your right side, you will simply turn left. Also, if Scruffy is lagging, you don't want to automatically drag him forward. This can be very intimidating. Instead, slap your leg as you use words of encouragement. If this doesn't do the trick, then you will **have** to tug down and forward. Make sure you tug and release. Never, **ever** pull!

1. Begin by giving Scruffy the Sit command. Now you have his attention. Place yourself at his right side, making sure you are positioned between his head and shoulders.
2. Show him the bait, first by putting it near his nose and then drawing your left hand near your knee. (Should you be working with a toy breed, you may want to lower your left hand to your calf. With a large

Whenever your dog forges ahead, pull down as you turn right.

Left: Proper heeling position. Middle: Begin the Heel on your left leg, but keep your target low enough for your puppy to follow. Right: Begin on your left leg as you say, "Scruffy, Heel."

breed, bring your hand up to your hip.) Say "Scruffy, Heel," as you step forward on your left leg. As soon as he responds and walks with you, praise him.

3. Walk three to five steps. Praise him from the moment he responds. Stop and tell him to sit. As soon as he sits, give him his reward. Repeat, adding a few more steps each time before stopping.

Once you can perform at least twenty steps of forward-moving heel, it's time to incorporate turns. In fact, should Scruffy try to pull ahead at this point, you should do turns to regain his attention.

As you add steps and turns you can put the bait away and bring it out only **after** Scruffy sits. Now, with your left hand free, you can put it on the leash, palm downward. Allow eight to twelve inches of leash

between where it attaches to Scruffy's head halter and meets your left hand. Continue to hold the loop of the leash and any extra leash in your right hand. Use your left hand for tugging downward when doing a correction. If Scruffy is a medium or small dog, you will need to bend both at the knees and at the waist as you tug down. Do not stop when you tug during the Heel. Part of your leverage depends on remaining in motion.

Remember the timing part in all this? Proper timing of your corrections is essential in teaching Scruffy where he is supposed to walk with you. You need to be consistent with his positioning. The more consistent you are, the faster he'll understand and the better he'll respond. As soon as Scruffy is only inches away from your target area—his head to shoulder region even with your left leg—you need to correct and bring him back into position. (You'll be able to tell if you see his ears in front of your left leg.)

The ultimate time to make a correction is when Scruffy is **about** to move out of position. You'll know this by keeping an eye on his head position. Should his head move to the left, do a quick right turn. Allowing him to remain more than six inches from your side or moving in front of you will make all future training more difficult. This is inconsistent and will be frustrating for both of you—for him because you'll be constantly correcting him and for you because you'll be constantly pulling. Start off being consistent, and everything will go smoother.

Use your voice simultaneously with your physical reprimand of pulling down. Say "No!" (or whatever word you are using) in a low tone of voice. Remember not to use his name with your reprimand and don't draw the word out or repeat. It's not "no, no, no" or "Noooo." A simple quick and firm "No!" will do, sharp and low toned. Eventually, all you'll need is your verbal reprimand to correct him. Imagine, Scruffy being on complete vocal control! That's the ultimate goal.

Probable Scenarios

Scenario 1: You are walking forward in the Heel. Scruffy moves ahead of you. You are to tug down and back as you say, "No!" You can also do a 180-degree turn to the right as you pull down and say, "No!" This works very well with a large dog.

Scenario 2: You are walking forward in the Heel. Scruffy moves to the left. You are to turn right and tug down and to the right as you say, "No." Continue walking. Don't stop and wait or look at him. Remember, you'll feel on the leash whether or not he's with you.

Scenario 3: You are walking forward in the Heel. Scruffy comes around to your right side. Turn left and continue walking. Voila! Scruffy is back on your left side. No leash work required!

Scenario 4: Scruffy is walking with you but is not in proper heeling position. He's a foot or more behind you. Slap your left leg and say, "Come on, boy!" in an enthusiastic tone of voice. When he catches up, praise him. If he doesn't, then tug down and forward in short bursts until he does catch up.

Granted, you want to walk fast and do many quick turns when training, but you will also need to make special considerations for dogs with short legs. You cannot go the same speed with a Corgi as you would with a German Shepherd Dog. It's not fair. Adjust yourself accordingly.

How to hold the leash when not using bait.

Distractions and Dilemmas

We are now at a point where Scruffy is heeling and sitting at our side when we stop. He turns with us most of the time and is watching, enjoying his praise, and eagerly awaiting his reward. What happens when Scruffy is suddenly faced with a distraction? Another dog wanders into the area, or a squirrel decides to venture closer to watch his nemesis working. Suddenly, Scruffy starts lunging and maybe even barking.

Don't fret! First of all, Scruffy won't be able to lunge very well while wearing a head halter. All it takes is either a few smooth forward and upward pulls to make him sit, or a downward and backward tug and release to maintain his heeling to regain his attention. Much easier than having to choke a dog that's dragging you down the sidewalk, right? Scruffy cannot put his weight into his lunge. All you need to do is continue walking, do your turns, and ignore the distraction.

Should he not listen to coaxing, pull down and forward as you do a 180 degree turn in a quick motion to lift his rear off the ground and make him move with you. Do not drag him.

Remember when I mentioned that you are Scruffy's leader? He **will** follow his leader. Should you react to the distraction, you can bet on it that Scruffy will as well. You need to fully ignore the distraction and teach Scruffy that he is to do the same. A few turns and you'll have his complete attention again. He may watch the other animal from the corner of his eye, but will not lunge after it. Your tug on the head halter says, "Relax, I'm in control." Don't forget that.

Always try to coax your dog to listen, instead of forcing.

Should Scruffy be older than five months, he'll have a lot of avoidance games up his furry sleeves. It won't take him long to learn that you'll stop and react to any one of them. These games include the following: Planting his rear, laying down, pulling back, rubbing the head halter on your leg or the ground, and jumping up at you. They are all disruptive and can become frustrating. Don't think for a moment that Scruffy doesn't realize this. Dogs are born trainers. They know how to get the upper paw. They know how to reach their people's breaking points. The moment you throw your hands up in desperation, Scruffy's got your number. He's saying to himself, (in doggy terms of course), "Aha! All I have to do is persevere until I get my way." Avoid this by being persistent and never giving in no matter what is going on around you. Instead of Scruffy feeling smug about his success, he'll be saying, "Well, I guess I can't get away with that." And he'll challenge you less and less.

Let's take these doggy games one at a time. First of all, planting the rear. Scruffy decides he's going to call the shots and that it's time to sit and get his treat. You might think, "It's so cute that Scruffy anticipated stopping." Don't fall for it! Keep moving. Try by first slapping your leg with the enthusiastic encouragements. If he remains, tug and release down and forward and do a 180 degree turn as you say "No!" He'll catch up.

Second, laying down. This is a tough one. You really don't want to drag Scruffy by the head. However, the worst thing you could do is stop and look at him. The best means of getting him up is to do a 180 degree turn and walk by your dog while you encourage him to catch up. After passing by him a few steps, he'll most likely get up. If not, crouch down and slap your leg. As soon as he gets up, offer him lots of praise and tell him to sit.

Should your dog lay down while doing a sit/stay, take a hold of his neck collar and lift him back up. The lift should be quick, not slow.

Some dogs will lay down when they are supposed to sit. If you have a small dog, put a hand under his chest and lift him into a sitting position. If your dog is larger than a Cocker Spaniel, take hold of the back of his regular neck collar and lift. Do this quickly, not slowly. As soon as his front legs are straight, release. Never pull a dog into a sit using the head halter. Should your dog lay down and then roll over onto his side you should not attempt to lift him into a sit. Instead, go forward one to two steps of Heel and then stop and tell Scruffy to sit. This will prevent Scruffy from turning it into a game of "Bite the Groping Hand."

Some dogs, especially those over the age of two years, while starting out well, will soon rebel about being told where to go and what to do. They will pull back. Again, don't stop and look at them. If the coaxing to catch up doesn't work, try doing a right about turn. The dog will be turned with you, moving him out of his sit position. Should

The No Jump Box.

this not work, tug down and forward and keep walking.

For those dogs not yet acclimated to the halter, rubbing the head on your leg or the ground is a very common problem. Scruffy may try to get it off by putting his nose on the ground while he walks. Some dogs will take advantage of a down stay by rubbing their faces on the ground. You can correct this by a quick upward tug and release. This type of correction also works for a dog that likes to sniff while working. A sniffing dog is not attentive. Every time the nose goes down, tug and release in an upward motion with a "No!" Head halters are the best thing to happen to owners of odor-loving dogs. Instead of constantly jerking on the dog's neck to get him to break his attention off an enticing smell, a simple tug up suffices. No pain and instant attention.

Jumping up at you can be difficult to solve while trying to teach your dog to heel. If you have a pocket and a small No Jump Box (see Chapter 17) you can shake it with your right hand whenever he jumps. However, this can be difficult to coordinate. The simplest means of curing the jumping is to step away to your right and continue walking. You can also make him sit every time he tries jumping on you. This is done with a forward and upward pull on the head halter as you say, "Scruffy, Sit." Another way is to tug the leash down and toward the left as you say "No!" Catching him in mid-flight with this correction is the most effective means of curing the problem.

You don't want to be correcting Scruffy for jumping on you when all four of his feet are on the ground, so the proper timing of your correction is very important. Use your reprimand while Scruffy's front feet are lifting off the ground, not when all four feet are touching the ground.

Be ready for anything. Scruffy will go through a learning plateau from time to time. Although this usually occurs while teaching the Down/Stay, it can happen anytime. The learning plateau is when a dog has learned something, but decides he'd rather pretend that he hasn't. This can continue from three days to two weeks. Be patient and persistent. Scruffy will soon learn that you will remain in control no matter what complications he presents. All dogs, even the best-trained ones, will challenge authority now and then.

Within a short time Scruffy will be walking with you. Both of you will enjoy your outings without any struggle or worry about whether or not the neighbor's dog is loose. Scruffy is at your side, prancing and grinning. The leash is loose and conversation pleasant. How can "Good boy" be anything but enjoyable?

Chapter 7

Stay for Me, My Darling

While teaching a stay may be difficult with a young puppy, it is one of the easier commands for an older dog. All Scruffy has to do is remain in one place and watch you walk around him. What's easier than that?

For Scruffy, the difficult part of this exercise will be remaining in one place when there are distractions. Scruffy needs to learn that no matter what happens, he must remain in the same spot.

You can allow him to move two parts of his body while he stays: his head to watch you and his tail to wag while you praise him. Even if he doesn't watch you the entire time, he is still performing what you commanded, provided he remains where you initially told him to stay.

There are three steps to a perfect stay: time, motion, and distance. For Scruffy to

perform reliably you will need to teach him each step using successive approximation. This term means that once your dog accepts a part of an exercise or, in this case, each stay command, you successively add more criteria.

We begin by teaching him to stay for up to a minute. Once he can do so, we teach him that he must remain as we walk around him in both directions. As he accepts remaining in one place with you walking around him, you can gradually increase your distance while you walk. Everything needs to be done gradually and each step built upon the previous one.

Actually, you already exercised successive approximation with the heel command. You started with one or two steps and, as Scruffy learned to remain at your side, grad-

As your puppy maintains his attention on the bait, tell him to Stay.

ually increased your steps. You also successively added turns to the exercise as well as a change of pace from time to time.

Think of it in these terms: Would you build a house without first putting in a foundation? No. It would not last. One big wind would knock it over. In the case of dog training, if you suddenly move away from Scruffy before he is ready, he'll constantly be breaking his stay command. He won't have a full understanding of the exercise, and both of you will become frustrated. You'll constantly be reprimanding him for something he doesn't understand. That isn't fair to either of you.

Instead, do one step at a time. Literally. Let's begin with teaching Scruffy to remain sitting for up to one minute.

1. Begin by heeling and doing turns and stops to get your dog's attention. Always

(left) Always step out on your right leg when teaching your dog to stay.
(middle). Stand before your dog close enough to touch his head.
(right) Say, "Scruffy, Stay," as you show your visual cue with your right hand.

begin with exercises Scruffy knows before continuing on to new things.

2. Stop and tell your dog to sit.

3. Transfer the entire leash into your left hand and put your right hand, palm facing Scruffy, fingers spread wide, in front of his face. Do not touch his face. Only place the visual cue nearby so that he can see it clearly. Even if his head is slightly turned away from you, he can still see the visual signal. Dogs have very good peripheral vision.

4. Say his name and the command "Scruffy, Stay," as you place your visual cue in front of his nose.

5. Step directly in front of Scruffy, **right** leg first. You should end up toe to toe.

⁻ Do not step away from him. He'll be more likely to get up and come toward you if you are a few feet away than if you are directly in front of him, within reach.

6. Praise him by saying, "Good boy," using a happy and enthusiastic tone of voice. Remain only a few seconds. Then return to his side in heel position.

7. Give him a reward, such as a small piece of food, a pat on the head, or a special toy.

8. Wait a few seconds, then continue into the Heel.

Each time you repeat the stay command, add a few seconds onto his staying time. Begin with five seconds and by the end of the first training session you should easily be up to fifteen seconds.

If Scruffy tries to get up you will need to correct him by saying, "No!" and pulling forward and upward under his chin. This motion makes his rear end go down. As soon as his rear touches the ground, loosen the leash and praise him. If he is not exactly where you had him originally, repeat your stay command.

Try very hard to make sure Scruffy is returned to where he was when you originally told him to stay. This is very important because if he gets the idea that he can move a little bit, he'll be shuffling around during his stays and not meeting the requirements of the exercise.

By the end of four or five days, Scruffy should be doing a stay for up to a minute. This may take a little longer for a very young dog—under five months—or one that is very old, such as over eight years. The younger dog has problems remaining still for a long time, and the older dog has problems accepting your authority after being the boss most of his life.

The time has come for step number two: motion. Once again, you must use successive approximation. Each time you do a Stay exercise, you will gradually increase your movements.

1. Work with your dog a few minutes and make him do a few long Stays with you standing in front of him.

Eventually, your puppy will maintain his stay without your visual cue or use of bait.

2. On the third or fourth Stay, begin to step side to side as he remains seated in front of you.

3. Return to Heel position, pause approximately ten seconds, praise, reward, then continue into your heeling work.

4. On the next Stay, take two steps to each side. Then return to Heel position, pause five to ten seconds, praise, and continue on.

5. The next Stay, take one step along each of Scruffy sides. You'll be going from one side to the other in a U shape.

6. Finally, when Scruffy remains motionless as you move along either side, walk completely around him before returning to Heel position. Remember, Scruffy must accept each motion before you continue on to the next movement. Should he not relax as you walk from side to side, do not begin going around him.

7. Now that Scruffy remains sitting and watches you as you move around him, go both ways. This

Gradually increase your distance by spiraling out.

has many purposes, the most important of which is to keep you from getting dizzy. Second, he needs to accept your moving around him in both directions.

Remember to praise him the entire time he stays. Scruffy needs reinforcement throughout his good behavior. The instant he pops up he hears, "No!" in that low, growly tone of voice. When he is back in place, he again hears "Good boy."

Offer Scruffy a recess after five minutes. You can release him from any position—Heel, Sit, or Stay. Just make sure he is performing the behavior correctly before you tell him, "Break."

We have now completed two parts of the stay exercise. The finale has arrived. It's time to add distance to the exercise.

1. Begin with the heeling and Sit/Stay exercises with which Scruffy is familiar.

2. While you walk around your dog, gradually increase your distance, one to two feet at a time on each stay exercise. Continue to spiral around Scruffy as you do so. Do not go straight out to the end of your leash. Spiraling out will make the increase of distance less noticeable.

3. Within five stays you should be able to make it out to the end of your six-foot leash. Do not get overly smug and drop your leash. This can be a major mistake. You'll have no means of making sure Scruffy remains in his stay, ruining the entire process.

Once Scruffy is remaining comfortably for a minute or more with you walking around him, it's time to expose him to distractions. Take him for a walk around the block. Or, if you can get a friend to help, have that person throw his toys around. Children are also a great distraction. They'll love to prove it to you as well. This has double benefits. Not only will Scruffy be tired after his training session, after running around, the children will all be pretty quiet too.

No matter how much Scruffy wants to get a toy or run with a child you must continue to maintain the status quo. Should he break his position, he is told "No!" then you pull forward and up on the halter, and he is replaced in the Sit/Stay. Then repeat your stay command, complete with visual signal.

According to you, nothing short of a natural disaster will allow Scruffy to break his stays. Be patient. Most dogs will learn within three to six replacements that they must listen no matter what is going on around them.

A light touch under the chin is helpful in teaching a submissive dog to remain in a Sit/Stay.

Tailoring the Training

Every dog is different. Some dogs will catch on to the stay exercise quickly, while others won't. All training needs to be tailored to the individual, so when it comes to procedures, nothing is written in stone. Some dogs can be insecure, while others will be very dominating. An insecure dog will not want to remain in one place while his owner moves away, whereas a dominant dog will be fine with his person moving away, but may not like having someone walking behind him.

When working with an insecure dog, it may help to touch him on his head or under his chin in the initial training stages. For example, when you are working on the first part of the Stay exercise, time, and are standing in front of Scruffy, place your hand under his chin and lift his head so that he is looking at your face. If he is so submissive that he doesn't want to look at your face, then touch the top of his head. You can even offer a little light rubbing as you touch his head. Dogs love being touched, so he'll learn that good things come to dogs who stay. When you get to the part when you are walking around him, continue to touch the top of his head as you move. This works as a stabilizer. He'll be less likely to pop up. As you progress to the distance work, he should be secure enough by then that you need to touch only occasionally.

If Scruffy does not like having people walking behind him, you need only take a little more time when working on the motion portion of the stay exercise. You can go along both his sides for a little longer and begin moving away from him before you do a complete circle. Scruffy may just dislike someone directly near his tail and will accept the exercise better if you are a little distance away before you walk behind him. Within a few training sessions he'll learn that nothing bad happens when you walk behind him and will become more comfortable with your proximity.

Daily Life

Now that Scruffy understands how to stay, you can incorporate the exercise into your daily routines, and by that I don't mean only training sessions, but everyday life. How often have you answered the door only to have him race through your legs, out the door, and into the street? What happens if someone leaves a gate open? Will Scruffy still be there? Do you have to hold your dog when someone comes into your home? How about at dinner time? Does he jump on you or sit staring at you with those big brown eyes?

All these things can be solved by Scruffy's learning how to stay. Before leaving through any door, Scruffy should perform a Stay exercise. Place him in a Stay, open the door or gate, Heel through, and then put him in a Stay on the other side as you close the aperture. This teaches Scruffy that the only way he goes through a door is in the Heel position. No more racing through your legs and out into the street. Practicing this with the yard gate is equally helpful. Scruffy will learn that even though the gate may be open, he must remain in his yard until you Heel him through.

To train this exercise, practice doing the stays near the openings. After opening the door, walk through and then back several times. Distraction proof by walking through and jumping around or throwing a toy through. Have other people walk through as Scruffy remains in a Stay. The ultimate distraction will be having another dog go through, especially a playmate.

If Scruffy is an exuberant greeter, you can teach him to remain in a Sit/Stay when people come into your home. Practice this by placing him in a Stay at the door **whenever** someone comes. No matter how long it takes, make sure he remains in his Stay as the person enters and the door is closed. Now, have that person allow Scruffy to sniff. The visitor should not touch him at this time. Scruffy needs to investigate to be sure that the visitor has good intentions. This changes him from an exuberant greeter into a wise, controllable watchdog. It is also a helpful exercise for dogs that go nuts every time someone comes to the door. They learn to control their wild urges. Wouldn't it be nice for Scruffy to automatically go to the door and sit when the bell rings? That is what this exercise will eventually accomplish.

As Scruffy progresses with his training you will be able to teach him to perform long Stays while you are busy with dinner or family activities, such as watching television or conversing with guests. This is best done through the use of a Down/Stay, which will be covered in the next chapter. A dog can only maintain a Sit/Stay for a short period of time, such as three to five minutes, whereas they can maintain a Down/Stay for up to an hour or more.

Chapter 8

Let's Relax

The down exercise tends to be one of the more difficult commands for a dog to accept. This is especially challenging for a dominant personality because it is equivalent to my commanding you, "On your knees before me." When dogs interact with each other, even in play, the more submissive dog will lie down when the dominant dog challenges. Some may simply crouch, while others will exhibit complete submission by rolling onto their backs and exposing their bellies. The former is called active submission, the latter passive submission.

As individuals, each dog will react to the Down command differently. A fear-aggressive dog may show active submission while growling and snapping. He is frightened, but not willing to entirely give in. A fully submissive dog will easily fall onto his back. Some may even urinate. (Submissive urination is very common in young dogs.) A dominant individual will protest being placed down by trying to wiggle away, pushing his weight against you, mouthing, or outright snapping. (If you have a dog with a dominant personality, before trying this exercise, please read on through Chapter 17.)

Regardless of Scruffy's personality, we have to teach him that he must go down on command. We don't want to fight with him or have to clean up a wet mess. He needs to learn that it is the natural way of things and that it can actually be a pleasant experience. You are the Alpha figure in the pack and he is the Omega. Once you have Scruffy going down on command, you have a dog that, with you at least, generally understands his own pack position.

The key to making this lesson more enjoyable and less of an exercise in submission (although that is really what it is to the dog) is to offer lots of praise and rewards. Does Scruffy enjoy having his tummy rubbed? Most dogs do. This can be incorporated into the exercise to make it more pleasant. The use of food rewards also helps.

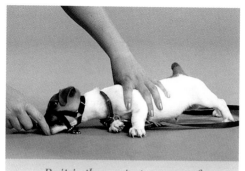

Bait is the easiest means of teaching a puppy or older dog to go down on command.

Before you know it, Scruffy will easily lie down on command because he knows it brings good things.

The easiest means of teaching your dog to lie down is through baiting him. After

Show your dog the target as you give the down signal and command.

practicing the exercises that Scruffy is familiar with for at least five minutes, stop and do the following:

1. Place the entire leash in your left hand. Hold it loosely. Scruffy will not be able to go down if you are holding the leash tight.
2. Hold a treat in your right hand between your thumb and middle finger.
3. Allow Scruffy to sniff the treat, then use your index finger to point at the ground directly under his nose. Say, "Scruffy, Down" in a demanding tone of voice. (Just be sure you are not using your reprimand tone.)
4. He will follow the smell of the treat and lower his head. Most dogs will completely lower themselves to the ground. If he doesn't . . .
5. As his head lowers, use your left hand on his shoulder blades (leash still in your left hand to be sure it doesn't become tangled in his legs) and apply a bit of pressure. The shoulder blades represent your dog's center of gravity. Pressure in this area will prevent Scruffy from wiggling out from under you or being able to counteract your weight.
6. As soon as Scruffy's belly touches the ground he has completed your request. Praise and reward him.
7. Before you release the pressure on his shoulder blades, transfer your leash into your right hand.
8. Remove your hand from his shoulders and go directly into the heel.

Had you been teaching a young puppy the Down during the Round Robin game, simply release the shoulder pressure and allow the next person to call him to Come.

Practice this exercise at least six times during your training session, or more, if you have

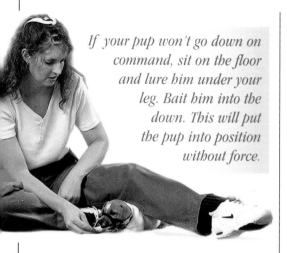

If your pup won't go down on command, sit on the floor and lure him under your leg. Bait him into the down. This will put the pup into position without force.

1. Stop and place the entire leash in your left hand.
2. Point down directly under Scruffy's nose as you say, "Scruffy, Down."
3. Should he not readily lower his entire body, put your left hand just behind his shoulder blades and apply a little pressure.
4. Using your right hand, take hold of his forelegs and bring them forward. Apply a little more pressure just behind his shoulder blades to keep his rear end from popping up.

If Scruffy is a puppy or small breed of dog you'll be able to fit both his forelegs into one hand. However, if he is a breed larger than a Spaniel, you'll have to use another method.

First, check to see which side he is leaning on. You'll be able to tell by looking at his hips. Whichever hip you see less of is the side on which he is leaning. Take the foreleg that bears most of his weight, bring it toward the middle of his body and forward. You will

the time. Be sure to vary your commands. Remember that Scruffy becomes pattern-trained very easily and will start to perform before you give a command, only because he knows what comes next.

To vary the exercises, do different things when you stop. For example, one time do a Sit/Stay, the next, do a Down/Stay. On the third round have him sit and then go directly into the Heel again. At one stop do both a Sit and Down/Stay. This keeps Scruffy on top of his game. He'll have to wait for his commands, thus becoming more attentive and less likely to anticipate.

While doing the Round Robin game with a young pup you can similarly vary the commands by having one handler do a Sit/Stay and the next do a Sit and Down combination. When the pup returns to handler number one, that person simply has Scruffy Junior come and sit, and so on.

If Scruffy doesn't care about a food reward, you will have to place him into the Down position. This should be done gently but firmly, keeping in mind his size and breed.

When your pup arrives and sits, bait him into the down and maintain slight pressure on his shoulder blades as you tell him to stay.

49

need to press him over toward the side he is leaning on, thereby using leverage to place him into the down position. This procedure should be easily accomplished provided you have chosen the correct side.

If this is difficult, it means you have either, one, not chosen the correct side, or two, are pulling his foreleg away from his body instead of into it. Performing this incorrectly will cause Scruffy quite a bit of consternation, making him very rebellious about going down. Recheck your procedures and make certain that no matter how much Scruffy tries to wiggle out of going down, you definitely get him there. You must back up every command, or he'll learn to ignore you. Adding a pat on the chest once he's down will relieve much of his anxiety. Be patient and persistent.

Once Scruffy is relaxed while he's down, you can begin working on the Down/Stay. Since he's already learned to do this in the Sit, he'll pick up on it very quickly. There are a few differences when teaching the Down/Stay versus the Sit/Stay. Yes, we begin with time, then motion, and finally distance,

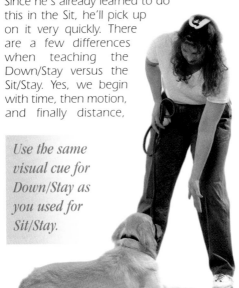

Use the same visual cue for Down/Stay as you used for Sit/Stay.

Should your dog not go down on command, put pressure on the shoulder blades with your left hand, and bring his legs forward with your right.

but we do not step in front of Scruffy while doing the time portion. Instead, remain at his side and work your way into standing upright. Working your way means releasing the pressure on his shoulder blades and reducing the tummy patting to the point where you can remain upright at his side without his moving. Gradually increase the amount of time he remains down before stepping forward into the Heel.

When working on the motion procedure, begin your motion by moving along his right side. Take a step in each direction as you did with the Sit/Stay in front. Be certain to never lead your motion with your left leg. All Stays begin with your right leg. With each

If your dog refuses to go down on command or is a very dominant dog, put pressure on shoulder blades as you pull downward on the halter.

ing a complete circle around him could take anywhere from one session to several weeks. Every dog is different.

Increasing your distance will be easy once Scruffy is relaxing in his Down/Stay as you circle around him. Simply add a foot or two of distance as you move around him on each successive Down/Stay exercise. Any time he pops up immediately say, "No!" and replace him. First, return him to his same spot. Second, place him into position, putting him into a Sit with a forward and upward pull on the head halter and then placing him in the down with the same procedure previously utilized. Repeat your Stay command.

After having to do this (replace Scruffy in the Down) for several weeks, without Scruffy going down on command, you'll need to firm up your reprimand. The head halter will make this an easy correction.

Down/Stay exercise, gradually increase the number of steps in each direction.

As Scruffy accepts your moving along his side, your next motion is to step behind him and up to his other side. Dogs are less likely to move out of their Down/Stays when you are stepping behind them rather than stepping in front of them. Continue with this exercise on each Down/Stay command. In a few training sessions, you'll be able to make a complete circle around Scruffy. Take your time. Scruffy must become reliable on each portion before going on to the next, otherwise, he will not fully understand the meaning of Down/Stay. Accomplish-

Walking over your dog while he stays is a good distraction proofing exercise.

1. After replacing Scruffy into the same spot in a sitting position, place the entire leash in your right hand.
2. Put your left hand on his shoulder blades.
3. Pull downward on the head halter as you apply pressure to his shoulder blades. Continue the pressure until Scruffy's tummy touches the ground, then immediately stop the pressure and tell him, "Scruffy, Stay."

This procedure can also be used for dominant dogs, which are usually extremely reluctant about going down. The aforementioned procedure will allow you to place him into position without the danger of being mouthed. The head halter will keep his jaws away from your hands as well as applying those pressures that say, "Listen, I'm in charge."

Once Scruffy can perform the Down/Stay with you walking around him, six feet away, you can begin distraction-proofing. Start with his toys and advance to people and other dogs. Each time he pops up, you simply replace him as you have been doing. Remain calm and Scruffy will know you are in control. If you become nervous, Scruffy will think he has no leader and must assume the role.

Never take your eyes off of him to watch the distraction. Your distraction is his distraction. It isn't only your eyes that will relate this. Your very thoughts will be conveyed to him through your odor. Dogs are very sensitive at

It is far better to teach your dog to do a down/stay at the door than to let him bark and jump around when he hears the mailman or the doorbell rings.

discerning emotions through their terrific sense of smell. Scruffy will know your state of mind before you realize you're feeling it.

Don't forget to give Scruffy a break every five to seven minutes. This will help him remain in a positive state of mind and maintain a higher level of attentiveness for a longer period of time.

Down/Stay Activities

Once Scruffy can perform the Down/Stay you can use it as a means of teaching him to relax in many different situations. Should he become upset during thunderstorms, you can desensitize him by placing him in a Down/Stay while playing a recording of banging sounds. As he remains in a Stay, gradually turn up the volume. As long as he remains, he is praised. If he gets up, Scruffy is returned to his Stay. Practicing this exercise every day may soon have your dog fully accepting the loud, booming noises and relaxing when the next thunderstorm passes over. However, some dogs do not respond to the desensitization process and will forever be afraid of the thunder. You can try to encourage these dogs into a positive state of mind through involving them in a fun activity, or simply working with them in the house as the storm rages outside, taking their mind off of the scary thing and onto something positive.

The Down exercise can be used on dogs that charge the door at the sight of the mailman. When Scruffy runs to the door, instead of allowing him to go crazy, make him perform a Down/Stay. This will calm him down and cause the mailman to give a sigh of relief. This technique can also be used when the doorbell rings or someone knocks.

The Down/Stay is also a means of teaching a dog to not beg at the dinner table. He is simply put in a Down/Stay on a nearby mat or blanket. This avoids your having to reprimand him every time he jumps up or begs. The more you can avoid having to reprimand, the more positive your relationship with Scruffy.

Sometimes traveling with Scruffy can be difficult. Say he leans out the window, jumps into the front seat, and tries to sit in your lap. These are all dangerous behaviors while you're trying to concentrate on the road. In the beginning of training your dog to remain in the back seat, you'll need to enlist the help of a family member or friend. Have them drive while you make sure Scruffy maintains his Down/Stay. As Scruffy progresses, he'll learn to remain in his Down/Stay while **you** drive.

The Down/Stay can be utilized while relaxing in the family room or when conversing with guests. Should Scruffy enjoy chasing children, placing him in a Down/Stay while they run about can prevent many accidental knockdowns. Also, there are many children who are afraid of dogs. They may accept Scruffy lots easier if they greet him while he remains in a Down/Stay.

The use of a head halter during the down exercises and, in fact, all training procedures, will surely turn that canine lion into a puppy lamb, giving you the upper paw.

Chapter 9

Come to Me,
Beloved

Of all the things you'll be teaching Scruffy, the most important is for him to come when he's called. In order for him to respond 100 percent of the time, he must know that he'll receive something very positive when he arrives. His reward can be a treat, toy, or your open arms with promises of petting and affection.

To communicate to your dog that he's got good things awaiting his arrival, he must never be called to come and then punished—**no matter what he did wrong.** This is true whether you chased him for two hours and panicked every time he ran into the street or found a mess that he made prior to your coming home. Even if you finally catch up to him, and he comes to you the last two feet, Scruffy must know that coming is the best thing in the world that he could

ever do. Provided the command remains positive, you'll soon have a dog that comes to you at all times, no matter what's going on around him.

Most dogs will naturally respond to the appropriate body language and visual cues. Very rarely will you have to drag your dog to you. This only happens when there is an irresistible distraction, such as another dog or a piece of food. After training Scruffy the Come command, you can proof him against these types of distractions, teaching him to ignore everything but your desire for him to come.

Dogs are very attracted to pleasant things, such as play or treats. Therefore, the best way to teach Scruffy to come is by presenting these things. However, because you won't always want to carry treats around, we need to simultaneously teach Scruffy to

Come to Me, Beloved

Bend forward at the waist as you say, "Scruffy, Come."

not consist of his coming to you, but rather your going to him. Who's training whom?

Ideally, Scruffy should sit facing you, not on your feet or looking back to where he came from. For him to learn to sit quickly and, eventually, automatically, when he arrives, he'll need to receive another visual cue from you. When he gets close stand upright. He will look up at your face, which will cause his rear end to go down.

As with other training exercises, you don't want Scruffy to learn a pattern. This is easily done through performing a command in only one way. Practice the come from Sit/Stays, Down/Stays and from break time. Call him from in front, behind, and off to either side. If Scruffy is proficient at performing his stays while you are out of sight, then do the come also from out of sight. Always at the end of your six-foot leash, of

respond to something you will always have—your voice and body movements.

When calling your dog to come, bend at the waist, to make yourself look more inviting. As he nears you, stand upright. If you are working with a puppy under the age of four months, you should crouch down when calling him to you. Also, give Scruffy the Come command in a happy tone of voice, never in a mean or low tone. The lower frequencies will warn him away instead of toward you. The happy tone will be an invitation: "I'm here. Come and get good things."

Your goal on the Come (also called the Recall) exercise is for Scruffy to make a beeline for you and to sit facing you. He should be close enough for you to touch easily without having to bend over (unless, of course, he's a very small dog). You should never have to adjust yourself to his head. For example, Scruffy is coming, but he will not end up in front of you, so you move to the side to accommodate where he will end up. This does

Your dog should sit facing you when he arrives.

course. This will prepare him for future training exercises.

1. Spend the first five minutes of your session
practicing exercises Scruffy already knows.
2. Do a Sit/Stay and walk around your dog.
3. Stop, turn, and face Scruffy.
4. Bend at the waist (or, with a young puppy,
crouch down) and say, "Scruffy, Come," in
an inviting, happy tone of voice.
5. As he walks (or runs) toward you, gather
up the leash so that he doesn't step on it.
Be careful to not pull on the leash. We
don't want to teach Scruffy to come only
when he's being dragged toward you.
6. When he is only a few feet from you,
stand upright.
7. As he arrives, say, "Scruffy, Sit." Be sure to
praise him as he is coming toward you
and after he sits. Give him a reward after
he completes his Sit. This can be a pat on
the head, a treat, or a toy. Be sure to not
touch him **until** he sits.

If Scruffy does not sit on command, do
not correct him by pulling upward as you
have done on the sit and stay exercises. This
would give him a bad message, such as,
"When I arrive, I'm corrected," and he will be
reluctant to come to you. Instead, place him
into the sitting position gently and continue
to praise him. Shortly, he will sit on command,
and very soon after that he will sit automatically without your having to say a word.

Distraction Proofing

A great place to practice the recall command is at a park where Scruffy might be
playing with other dogs. Every so often call
him to come, praise him, and then release

him again to go play. This will soon teach
Scruffy to come even when he's in the midst
of playing with other dogs, which can be the
most difficult time for a dog to respond to
the recall command.

If Scruffy finds a best friend that he does
not want to leave, you will need to go get
him and bring him back to where you called
him from. Praise him when he sits before you
and then release him again with the word,
"Break." You may need to practice doing this
every couple of minutes.

For the dog that will not respond to the
Come command regardless of your vocal
tone and body language, you will have to
tug and release as you reel him toward you.
As soon as he takes a step toward you,
praise exuberantly. Each time he hesitates or

*As your dog nears
you, stand upright.*

draws away from you, tug on the leash. The head halter will bring his head closer to you, thus making his body follow. Within a short time you will no longer have to do this reprimand, for Scruffy will quickly figure out what you want.

Once Scruffy comes to you immediately, you can begin distraction proofing. Have someone throw Scruffy's toys around. That person can also crouch down and clap their hands or pat the ground. In doggy language this means, "Come and play!" If you have a friend who owns another dog, have that person work with their dog nearby. Place the other dog in a stay along the same trajectory as you will be calling Scruffy to come.

Any time Scruffy tries to go toward the distraction, say, "No!" and give a light tug on the leash as you take a step or two backward. As soon as he's returned to his beeline, praise him and continue drawing in the leash.

Should your dog hesitate on his way to you, step backward.

Recall Games

Even if Scruffy is an older dog, you can play the Round Robin game with him. He'll thoroughly enjoy it and can also learn the names of family members and friends.

Begin by doing the recall and sit exercises. Once he's readily going to each of you in turn, begin naming the person he's to go to. When the person hears his or her name, that person calls Scruffy to come. Each time Scruffy arrives at his destination, he receives his rewards.

Next, he must learn to go to the named person without that person calling him to come. You say, "Scruffy, go to Mike." If he has heard this command repeated often enough, he'll know who you're talking about. In the beginning, Mike can crouch down to make himself more easily identified. Once Scruffy goes to and sits before Mike, then Mike should praise and then send him off on another errand, such as, "Scruffy, go to Cathy." This game teaches Scruffy many different skills. One, of course, is coming to different people. Another is to go find specific people. After Scruffy acquires these skills indoors, try teaching it to him outdoors. You can increase the parameters of the exercise by having the person Scruffy was sent to see hide behind something, such as a hedge.

Did you have any idea that you were teaching the initial stages of search and rescue work? Even if you don't want to train your dog in this, it's still a fun game that can be played by the entire family, both two- and four-legged alike.

Chapter 10

Stand for the Doctor

The Stand exercise is a very important part of teaching Scruffy to behave. It is often used in the show ring both in conformation and obedience. The dog must stand and stay while being examined by the judge.

This is but one of many possible uses for this exercise. It was originated for a more profound purpose—remaining immobile for a physical health examination.

Dogs out in the field are prone to injury and parasite infestation. Remaining in a Stand/Stay allows their handlers to investigate an injury and to rid their dogs of parasites before going home. No one wants to bring ticks and other bugs into their home or kennel.

Trying to do this on a squirming dog makes for inaccurate examinations. However, a dog that remains in one place, all four feet square, allows his handler to be more efficient.

Applications of the Stand/Stay

Every veterinarian loves a patient that remains still and cooperative throughout health examinations. A trained dog is a gem. Scruffy can maintain a Stand/Stay while having his abdomen examined, do a Sit/Stay while having his ears, eyes and neck checked, and a Down/Stay while the doctor draws blood. Not only does this make the entire affair easier on the doctor, it also makes it easier on Scruffy.

Remaining under some type of command allows Scruffy to relax. He knows what is happening. He knows someone is in charge of the situation. Besides, while learning the Stand/Stay, he gets a lot of tummy rubbing. No dog would turn that down! The positive associations with the teaching of this exercise, coupled with his knowledge of his environment, allows you an easy doctor visit every time.

Once Scruffy learns this exercise, not only can he perform for his doctor, he can also make bathing far easier. As with a wiggly dog during examinations, you don't want a wiggly dog during bathing, or you end up wetter than your dog. Again, you can use the different stay positions to your advantage when doing a tub bath.

Begin with a Down/Stay to wet him all over. Go to a Stand/Stay while soaping and

Place your entire leash into your right hand. Sweep your left hand from his nose . . .

another Down/Stay to rinse. The Sit/Stay will come in handy while drying his head, neck, and front sections, while a Stand/Stay aids in drying his hind end. You end up with a clean dog who is relaxed with the entire process and, best of all, you remain mostly dry.

Training Procedures

There are two ways to teach the Stand/Stay. One is from a sitting position and the other while heeling in motion. The head halter is not used much in this exercise (unless Scruffy tries to forge ahead of you or go toward a distraction) because if you were to pull up on it, Scruffy would think he must sit, the opposite of what we want him to do. All commands and manipulations are done through vocal and visual cues. Touch, in the form of a tummy rub, will play a large part as well. This will help Scruffy relax and enjoy the stand exercise.

As always, begin every training session by working on exercises that are familiar. It normally takes five minutes for any dog to settle into fully attentive patterns. Give him a short break and then continue on to new lessons.

1. After you have stopped and Scruffy is in a sit at your side, place the entire leash into your right hand. Your fingers should be touching the stitching that attaches the clip to the leash. Thus, it is fairly tight, but do not use it at this time.
2. Spread the fingers of your left hand and place your open palm even with Scruffy's nose. Do not touch him, simply present the visual cue.
3. As you say, "Scruffy, Stand," sweep your left hand from his nose to his haunches. Stop just short of his hind leg and reach under his tummy.

4. Press lightly on his solar plexus. This is at the base of his rib cage and is a very tender area, so don't press hard.

5. As you press, **now** pull forward **gently** on the leash. You won't need to exert much pressure there, either. In fact, if you do, Scruffy will not stand up, he'll remain sitting, for the pressure will be similar to the correction for leaving a Sit/Stay.

6. When Scruffy stands, rub his tummy and praise him.

Gradually increase the amount of time that he remains standing at your side. Should he move any of his legs, use your reprimand word and physically move the leg back in place. It is very important that you rub his tummy continuously as you praise. This will prevent him from wanting to move forward.

When Scruffy is steady on this exercise, you can proceed with teaching him how to stay. However, he must be at a point where he is able to stay still for upwards of thirty seconds.

1. Once you have him in the Stand, continue to rub his belly with your left hand.

2. Place the leash between your knees and present your stay signal with your right hand as you say, "Scruffy, Stay."

3. Retrieve your leash with your right hand and place a finger or two of your right hand through Scruffy's regular neck collar (see page 62). This will control his front end, should he try to move forward. Do not apply any pressure here unless he moves. If he does so, tug back on the neck collar and immediately release. Keep in mind that should you continue to apply pressure, Scruffy will also continue to pull against you. All physical reprimands are tug and release, never a pull.

4. Gradually increase the amount of time Scruffy remains in that position.

When your dog can remain in a Stand/Stay for near a minute, begin using your left hand to examine him in areas other than his tummy. Move your hand along his side, then down his legs. His back and then his head and ears are next. This prepares him for the veterinarian checking him all over. Be sure to look in his ears, lift his lips to check his teeth, and lift his tail to prepare for the inevitable thermometer.

. . . toward his tail as you say, "Scruffy, Stand." Pull forward gently as you lift your dog under his tummy.

Stand for the Doctor

Now that Scruffy remains standing while being examined, he needs to learn to do so without your constantly touching him and also allow you move away from the Heel position.

1. Place Scruffy in a Stand/Stay.
2. While touching him with your left hand, move behind him. By now he should be reliable enough for you to let go of his neck collar.
3. Move around to his left side and then back to heel position.
4. Go forward into your heel. Always go from a stand to a forward-moving heel. Later, you can vary the exercise to include having him sit or lie down from a Stand.

While first teaching Scruffy how to do this exercise, never have him do a recall from the Stand/Stay. He'll already be very eager to anticipate this command because he knows that very good things happen when he comes. If he begins anticipating, you might have to return to square one on the Stand exercise to improve his reliability.

5. Perform the Stand/Stay a few times in this manner. You go from his right side to his left side and return to his right side.
6. As Scruffy becomes reliable on this, the next step is to cross in front of him. Remember, you are touching your dog the entire time as you walk around him.
7. When Scruffy performs this part of the exercise well, then it's time to vary the touching. Take a few steps without touching, then return to touching.

Continue to phase out your touch as you proceed with this exercise. It could take anywhere from four days to two weeks before Scruffy can remain standing with you walking completely around him without touching him. At this time you can begin to increase your distance as you walk around. Do so very gradually. Should Scruffy break from his position, physically return him to the same place he was told to stay. Always use your verbal reprimand the second he moves away. Don't wait until he's coming toward you. This can become confusing for him. All reprimands must be done at the exact moment of the misbehavior.

Scruffy may be a very large breed, in which case you may want to begin the Stand exercise from the active heeling motion. This way you won't have to do any lifting—he's already up. However, your timing has to be impeccable.

Put a finger through the neck collar as you rub your dog's tummy.

As Scruffy becomes reliable on the Stand/Stay, you can cross in front of him.

Be sure to vary the exercises. Sometimes have Scruffy stop and sit and other times, stop and stand. This teaches him attentiveness versus pattern training.

Once you have Scruffy standing comfortably, you can proceed with the elongation of the Stand/Stay in the same manner as already discussed. You begin with touching and walking around, then move to the variable touch as you walk and eventually the increase of distance.

Guess what? You and Scruffy have passed basic obedience!

He now knows all the different positions and how to stay in them. He performs his commands regardless of what is going on around him and, best of all, he was never hurt throughout the entire process.

Again, begin with the exercises that Scruffy is familiar with.

1. As you are preparing to stop, place the entire leash into your right hand.
2. Spread the fingers of your left hand and position the palm to face the left side of Scruffy's head.
3. As you stop, say, "Scruffy, Stand," sweep your left hand from his nose to his haunches, and place your left hand in front of his left hind leg. This will effectively stop him.
4. As soon as he is stopped, begin rubbing his tummy.
5. After several seconds, continue on in your Heel.

Place leash between your knees; keep left hand under Scruffy's tummy; use your right hand for the Stay cue.

Chapter 11

We're Almost There

Every dog, regardless of breed, can learn to listen off-leash. This does not mean that, once you have completed this training, you can automatically walk him without a leash in public places. There are leash laws that must be followed. However, it does mean that you can expect your dog to listen without a leash while you are in a fenced yard at home or visiting a park where dogs are allowed to play together. Wildlife management areas are a great place to work with Scruffy off-lead. Because these are hunting areas and most hunting dogs work off-lead, Scruffy will be allowed to run around—provided he remains under control. A really well-trained dog will have more opportunity to exercise. Scruffy's absolute obedience will offer you a chance to unwind and enjoy your time with him.

Before taking off the leash, you need to prepare Scruffy for the transition. The prerequisites include his watching you at least 90 percent of the time. It would be nice to reach 100 percent, but we're not training him to be a robot, just a well-behaved dog. Most important is that he responds on one command, regardless of distraction.

Always expect the best from him and you will get it. This means that you should never adjust your pace to his or move to where you think he'll end up. Expect him to do this on his own. By now, he should know how.

Eventually, all of your off-lead communication will be through body language and verbal tones. You'll need to be precise in your actions, and your timing must be impeccable. Without this, Scruffy will become sidetracked, and you risk losing his attention.

We begin our off-lead preparation by using more vocal and visual cues than leash cues. This means doing many sharp, erratic turns and sudden stops. These exercises will teach Scruffy to watch you very closely because he won't know what you are going to do next. He'll also enjoy this immensely.

It's a game of follow the leader. It's not rare for dogs working in this manner to grin and strut. They love the challenge.

If, when you stop, Scruffy moves to sit in front of you instead of at your side, you will execute a Finish. This exercise will teach your dog to return to heel position, should he not already be there. Thus, it is used as a form of correction without actually having to tug on the head halter or verbally reprimand the dog. Scruffy simply learns that should he overshoot, he's to go behind your back and sit at your left side.

The Finish is also used after your dog comes and sits before you. Say, for example, that Scruffy is playing at the park. You are ready to leave. You call Scruffy to come and he arrives and sits in front of you. You can't step forward because to do so would mean either climbing over Scruffy or, if he's a small dog, tripping over him. Instead, you do your Finish. He moves himself into heel position and

During the initial stages of off-lead you are to perform the Heel exercise with an always loose lead.

By this time your dog should sit automatically without any leash usage or command.

you're clear to step forward. Scruffy is safely at your side and watching every movement.

The Finish can be a tricky exercise in that you must time your verbal and visual cues well. If you perform correctly, Scruffy will too, for he already knows this exercise. It's the heel, only in reverse!

The Finish can be done one of two ways. Scruffy may be one of those extremely bright dogs, and so he can learn both ways, using one or the other depending on the situation. Some dogs will have preferences. For example, many Dobermans and Shelties prefer to Finish to the left, while many other breeds prefer it to the right. A Finish to the right will have Scruffy moving back along your right side, walking behind you, and seating himself near your left leg. A Finish to the left is executed with Scruffy walking down your left side, turning left, and sitting at your left leg.

The command for performing either of these exercises is heel. Why, you ask, is Heel used again? Essentially because you are telling Scruffy to return to Heel position. You can use another command, such as Place, Swing, or anything else you want. In fact, you can use any word you want for any of the exercises, praise, reprimand, or release cue—simply use it consistently. Using a different word for the same exercise, which the forward Heel and Finish are, is just one more word Scruffy has to learn. Once he has a full understanding of each exercise you can add words with more subtle meanings, such as using Wait for a Stay that will include a Come at the end of it and using Stay when you plan on returning to Scruffy's side. Your dog already knows what Heel means so until the time he fully understands the Finish exercise, he'll learn it faster if you use what he already knows.

We'll begin with the Finish to the right.

Whenever your dog becomes distracted or inattentive, do an about turn.

1. Practice heeling with quick turns and stops.
2. When Scruffy stops in front of you, put only half the leash (that's two to three feet) in your right hand. The remainder of the leash should be between you and your dog.
3. Say, "Scruffy, Heel," as you take a big step back on your right leg. Be sure to move your right hand evenly with your right leg—in tandem. Moving your hand,

speaking, and moving your leg together are very important.

Scruffy will see the movement and understand immediately that he is to walk with the moving leg. He'll walk toward your right heel.

It's very important at this point that your leash is very loose. A tight leash will prevent Scruffy from getting up; to him a tight leash means a reprimand for not sitting. Besides, we're trying to teach him to listen off-lead and to pull as you give a command is contradictory to your goals.

Should Scruffy be distracted and not execute the command, try again. If it

happens again, then you should give a down and backward tug and release, along with your verbal reprimand. Remember, all physical reprimands must be in the opposite direction of Scruffy's incorrect movement or, in this case, no movement.

4. As soon as his body is even with your stationary left leg, bring your right leg forward until it is even with your left.

The timing of this is very important because if you keep your right leg stretched out, Scruffy cannot get around it. He'll either stand and wait for it to move, or sit, because he has learned that when you stop, he is to sit. If you don't

Step back on your right leg as your give the command.

Switch your leash behind your back into your left hand as you bring your right leg forward.

bring your right leg forward quickly enough Scruffy will, again, sit behind you.

5. As you bring your right leg even with your left, pass the entire leash behind your back into your left hand, bringing your left hand even with your left leg.

Scruffy will see that he is no longer even with your moving leg and will come to sit at your left side where he belongs. Should he not sit automatically, give him the Sit command and make sure he follows through.

If Scruffy lags behind your left side or sits before he reaches the appropriate destination, you should try slapping your left leg with your left hand and enthusiastically say, "Come on, boy," until he catches up.

Some dogs will overshoot their targets and continue in front of you. When this happens, do the Finish again. If after three Finishes, Scruffy stills overshoots, guide him into position at your side. You can guide the second time if you want, but some dogs just need to perform the exercise a few times to learn that they don't have to put in so much effort if they do it right the first time. Yes, many dogs **do** reason in this manner.

In many cases, it might help to tell your dog to sit when his right shoulder is perpendicular to your left heel. To be accurate in timing this, picture yourself as a clock, facing the twelve o'clock position. When Scruffy is in the seven o'clock position tell him to sit. That way, when he reaches the nine o'clock position, which is the proper Heel position, he'll be sitting. It normally takes the dog a few seconds to execute a command after you give it. (Picture the sound traveling into Scruffy's ear, into the brain, his deciding whether or not he wishes to comply, and then transferring signals down to his muscles. This can take a few seconds.) So giving the command at seven o'clock means that Scruffy will be sitting by nine o'clock. This prevents him from overshooting his mark. You are guiding with your voice, making the exercise easier for him. Granted, there are dogs that do react within a second of your command, such as those extremely intelligent, eager-to-perform Border Collies. If your dog is like this, go ahead and wait until he is close to the appropriate position before telling him to sit.

The Finish to the left should be done if Scruffy has a difficult time moving around

Bring your left leg back as you say "Heel," when doing a Finish to the left.

When your dog is even with your left leg, bring your leg forward.

As you draw your leash back to your side, your dog will attain a proper Heel position.

behind you. As previously mentioned, some dogs do have preferences.

1. Place half the leash in your left hand.
2. Say "Scruffy, Heel," as you take a big step backwards on your left leg and swing your left hand out to the side and back.
   Scruffy will get up and move along your left leg.

3. As soon as Scruffy's left shoulder is even with the heel of your left leg, step forward, bring your left arm into your body, and move it forward with your left leg.

Scruffy will turn to his left and move up with your left leg, sitting even with your left heel. Try to coax rather than pull your dog into position. Remember, pulling is counter-productive to off-lead training.

As you and Scruffy become adept at the finish you'll be able to reduce your visual cue for the behavior. Gradually decrease how much you bring your leg back as you give the command, but make sure to continue moving the leash around in the same manner. You need to do this anyway to prevent yourself from being entangled. Eventually, you'll be able to give Scruffy the Finish command without moving your leg at all.

The next step in off-leash preparation is to use your voice before utilizing a leash correction. This shouldn't be a problem at this point because you have always been using your vocal tones for guidance. The only difference now is that you'll be using a verbal reprimand **before** a leash correction. Should the verbal reprimand not work, then use it a second time with a **firmer** leash correction.

Keep in mind that with a head halter, properly executed leash corrections are not painful. It's similar to your mother telling you to go upstairs to clean your room and, if you don't comply, she takes you there. The indignity of it all will teach you that next time, you will go when she tells you to. Some dogs simply need a little more "push." Scruffy **will** learn to listen the first time.

Off-lead training is done in five phases. The first phase is teaching Scruffy to listen from a distance. You'll need a fifteen- to twenty-foot leash for this. Phase two will be the Fake Out phase. You'll be dropping the leash, but your dog won't realize he's off-lead. In phase three you'll be doing the same, but switching the leash to Scruffy's regular neck collar. At this point your dog will be doing his Stays and Comes using only his neck collar. Phase four will include an increase of distance and the reduction of leash presence. The leash will be dragging behind while heeling and be used solely for backup on the Stays and Comes if Scruffy gets a little distracted. Phase five is the big one. All Scruffy will be wearing is a little pull tab first on his head halter and eventually attached to his neck collar. After several months of practice the head halter comes off, and all you'll need is your voice and visual cues for complete control. You and Scruffy will be in sync and communicating.

Before starting these off-lead phases, be sure you have all your equipment.

1. The long leash
2. The pull tab
3. The regular tag-bearing neck collar
4. And of course, the head halter . . .
Here we go!

Chapter 12

I'm Still Here

Stage one of the off-lead process is deceptively easy, but important nonetheless. Some dogs will feel very insecure when you are further from them, while others will take it in stride. It's very important to do everything very gradually. Jumping ahead will ruin Scruffy's response stability.

Before beginning the first stage of off-lead training, practice increasing Scruffy's stay times. This is important because he will have to remain in place for upwards of two minutes during each off-lead stay in order for you to be able to increase your distance. As the two of you progress, stay times should increase.

Begin phase one of off-lead by practicing all of the basic obedience commands. Once Scruffy is settled into work, do a Sit/Stay and attach your long lead to his head halter. The long leash will be necessary because at times Scruffy will be sidetracked during his recall commands. An inviting stick,

a stranger to meet, or a dog to play with are all distractions that are sure to entice him. These are the reasons that we have a long leash.

Initially, the long leash will be difficult to organize, especially while doing a recall. Scruffy may come to you faster than you can gather the leash. It's natural that the further a dog is from his handler, the faster he'll come in.

Gather the leash by spreading your arms to the side as far as you can. This spreads the leash out. Then bring the two ends together into one hand and slide out again. Gathering in this manner is quick and efficient. It will also result in fewer knots.

Continue the exercise as before, only you will increase your distance from Scruffy by two feet. Since your regular leash was four to six feet, that means letting your long leash out to approximately six to eight feet. Each time you do a Sit/Stay or Down/Stay, add two feet to the distance as you walk around.

73

Spread your leash the full length of your spread arms.

Loop it and spread your arms again.

One word of caution: Do not go straight out to your set distance. Increase your distance as you walk around your dog. Otherwise, Scruffy will be less likely to remain in his Stay. Letting the leash out as you walk around, essentially spiraling out, will make your increased distance less noticeable.

Now comes the part where you must use the timing of your voice appropriately. Should Scruffy pop up, you don't want to be using your verbal reprimand as he's coming toward you. This would confuse him when

he performs his recalls. You must use your verbal reprimand when Scruffy is **thinking** of popping up—Scruffy's head will move forward and his body will tense. It's at this time that you say, "No!" in your low reprimand tone.

If you have to replace Scruffy, go directly to him (don't gather the leash first) and take hold of the leash within a foot of the head halter and guide him back into position. You must return him to the same location in which you had told him to remain to maintain the criterion of the exercise. Once you return him to the spot he was told to stay, pull forward and up to get him into a sit. If he gets up from a down stay, first replace him in a sit, then pull downward on the halter, also using your hands to press on his shoulder blades, until he is lying down. Repeat your stay command as you again begin to walk around him, gradually increasing your distance.

Should Scruffy break his stay position often, it means you need to return to remaining closer while doing the exercise. Take your time. Some dogs can be insecure and need to be reassured from time to time with a pat on the head or a treat to reinforce good behavior.

As you gradually increase the distance on your stay exercises, also incorporate the recall. For example, you have succeeded in having Scruffy remain in a stay at ten feet. Call him to come from that distance, and so on, incrementally increasing the distance of his recalls just as you are increasing the distance of his stays.

Scruffy may come and sit faster than you can gather the long leash. As he nears you, take hold of the leash within a foot of his head halter and guide (don't drag or pull) him into a sit before you. You can more easily guide him by stepping backward as he nears you while you gather the leash. Your movement will entice him to come to you. Once he's sitting, tell him to stay and then gather your leash.

Another way to handle this situation, should Scruffy's feet become entangled, is to take just enough leash (about three feet) from near his head halter to perform your finish. Once Scruffy is back in heel position, he is no longer entangled. Go directly into the heel exercise and gather the leash while walking. This will save you loads of time and

Hold all the extra leash in your right hand and allow at least a foot and a half of leash between you and your dog.

frustration, and you will need to utilize this method anyway when you get to the next phase of off-lead training.

Should Scruffy become distracted while coming, give the leash a tug and use your verbal reprimand. As soon as he is coming straight to you again, praise him enthusiastically. Essentially, what you are doing is guiding him with your voice. The entire time he is coming toward you, praise him. The second

When you do a Stay, gradually increase the distance, spiraling out.

Look inviting and gather your leash as your dog comes from a distance.

he veers off his beeline, use your verbal reprimand. Your voice is to be your leash.

As Scruffy becomes more reliable you can begin adding the Hide-and-Seek game to your training sessions. This game will teach your dog to maintain his stays while you are out of sight and to come to you when he can't see you. This exercise becomes more demanding during the next phases of off-lead training but is best begun when you are still holding that leash and thus have more control over the situation.

Take Scruffy to a parking lot or somewhere that has many trees, bushes, or other objects that you can hide behind. Practice your regular exercises until you have his complete attention. The first time you hide behind something, do so for only a few seconds as Scruffy remains in a stay. Continue to praise him as you hide. Come out again and return to walking around him. Each time you hide, do so for a little longer.

As Scruffy learns to accept the fact that he is to remain in his Stay, even when he can't make eye contact with you, you can begin to have him come to where you are hidden. Try to not do this on every Recall command, however, or Scruffy will anticipate the Come command each time you hide. He'll relate the fact that you are hiding with the inevitable command to come and, as soon as you are out of sight, he'll begin coming to you before you command him to do so. Remember, dogs are easily pattern trained. You must vary the exercises to keep them attentive.

It might help at this point to have someone watch Scruffy while you go out of sight and alert you if he gets up out of a Stay or does

not come when you call him. Otherwise, you'll need to peek around your hiding spot to check on him. You can be sure he'll see you. Dogs see movement very well, whether close up or at a distance.

Play the Hide-and-Seek game both outside and inside your home. Scruffy needs to learn to listen to you wherever you may be. Sometimes dogs will not listen as well in their play area as they do elsewhere. They need to learn that you rule **regardless** of your location.

Your leash should be gathered by the time your dog arrives and sits in front of you.

Chapter 13

Faked Out!

Until this point Scruffy has done everything on a leash. He is used to seeing something connecting you to him, which allows you to make sure he listens. Should he try to go after a ball, you can stop him. If he decides not to come, you can make him. Scruffy has identified the leash and head halter as your tools to back up commands.

Our goal is to teach Scruffy to listen without either a leash or a training device. Since the head halter has taught him that you are in charge, we should first phase out the use of the leash. Once Scruffy reliably obeys without any physical corrections, we'll phase out the head halter.

While reducing the use of the leash, be sure to not allow Scruffy to become sloppy. In fact, we must be extra diligent to ensure this doesn't happen. In Chapter 11, we discussed how to use leash reduction techniques and the Finish to correct a bad position. The leash reduction exercises must only be used when Scruffy is attentive. If he is distracted or in "one of those moods," then you'll **need** to use the leash correction with your "No!" more often. Sometimes one must regress in order to progress. This means that if Scruffy will not sit on command and still will not sit after a verbal reprimand, then you will need to use the leash to reinforce your command. If you don't, his response will become sloppy. In a short time Scruffy can learn your "No!" is weak (for you'll repeat it), or meaningless (you don't back it up).

While heeling, make sure Scruffy remains in the proper position—head even with your left leg. When you stop, he should sit automatically. Scruffy ought to be able to maintain a stay from up to twenty feet away with you hiding behind something. He should also be able to come **directly** to you without stopping to sniff or say hello to someone. Most of all, Scruffy should be able to do all these things with all types of distractions present. If this is not the case, strengthen any faults before continuing.

As you spiral out on the Stay, drop the leash.

1. Do a Sit/Stay command.
2. Walk around Scruffy and praise him.
3. As you walk, drop the leash. Yes, drop it! Do not lay it down. He'll see that body motion. Be nonchalant. As you walk put the leash behind your back and then just open your fingers and allow the leash to drop.
4. Continue walking around Scruffy. Never take your eyes from him.
5. When you return to the end of your leash, turn around and circle him in the other direction.
6. Return to the end of your leash, pick up your leash, and call Scruffy to come.

Provided Scruffy can perform all of his basic commands, including the stays and comes from up to twenty feet away, you are ready for this next level of dropping the leash. If you use appropriate body language, Scruffy will most likely not realize the leash has been dropped. He has learned to respond to your visual and verbal commands.

Begin your training exercises with the basic commands and increase the distances on the stays and comes as you practiced in the previous chapter. You should now be able to walk all the way around Scruffy at the end of your twenty-foot leash and call him from any direction. Work on this for ten minutes.

We are now into the prime training time, the five to ten minutes into the training session. It is always best to begin any new work during this time.

If at any time Scruffy popped up, say, "No!" in a low tone of voice, go directly to him, and replace him in the same spot. Do not take the time to pick up and gather the leash. Once he is returned, gradually work your way out again (the leash still on the ground) until you are twenty feet away and walking around him. This same correction is to be used if Scruffy anticipates his Recall command.

To reduce the incidence of anticipation, try to vary your body language while you walk around. For example, you probably tend to stop, look at Scruffy, and then lean forward as you say, "Scruffy, Come." There's nothing wrong with this visual cue. However, Scruffy has learned that when he sees you do this he will be called to come so he comes to you before you use the Recall word. He's not a bad dog, only jumping the gun a bit. As you'll recollect, dogs communicate largely with visual signals. You gave the visual cue for the Recall. He came.

You can teach him to wait for his command by pretending to place yourself in the Recall position but not calling him. If at any time he gets up, say, "No!" and put him back.

Try stopping every half or quarter circle and turn to face him. If Scruffy remains in his stay, praise him, then move on.

Moving around Scruffy at different speeds is also a great means of distraction proofing. Try walking slow, running, jumping, or skipping. Another great distraction is to crouch down and clap your hands. Most dogs will not be able to resist, but they must be taught to do so. For a dog to work reliably off-lead, he must be distraction proof.

As Scruffy remains in place on his Stays, begin to move a little further away as you walk around. Add just a foot or two every time you do the exercise. All the rules are the same. Scruffy must remain in the position you put him and the spot you left him in.

By the end of this prime training time you should be at least thirty feet distant on your Stays, and Scruffy should be coming directly to you from twenty feet, with you holding the leash and gathering as he comes.

Now return to the regular six-foot training leash and work him an additional ten minutes. The last ten minutes of a training session can be frustrating; Scruffy may be losing his attentiveness. Make the experience more positive by doing easier tasks, such as heeling with lots of turns and short distance Stays and Comes.

Although it may be more difficult to work your dog at this time, Scruffy needs to learn to listen for increasingly longer periods. A dog does not behave only twenty minutes a day. He needs to be able to respond at any time throughout the day. For example, should you wish to go for a walk with your dog, you don't want to be limited because Scruffy can only walk for twenty minutes. You need to gradually increase his walking time by taking him just a bit over his threshold. Add only a minute or two at a time, and soon he'll be working for thirty minutes or more without any problem.

To be sure you can back up your command, stand on the end of your leash prior to doing the recall.

Faked Out!

The next training session, Scruffy will learn to come without you holding the leash. This is the second "Fake Out."

Begin the training session, as before, with your long leash. Continue on to the point where you drop the leash and walk around. Remember to increase your distance beyond the reach of the leash while doing the Stay exercises.

1. When you return to the leash and prepare to call Scruffy to you, step on the end of the leash.
2. Call Scruffy with the same exact verbal and visual cues. Many people, now that their hands are free, have tendency to slap their legs. Don't do that. With your goals of having Scruffy come when he doesn't see you, the last thing you want to establish is another visual cue with the Recall command. He must learn to come on the verbal command alone. He already has a visual cue of your leaning forward that we must phase out.
3. As Scruffy approaches, praise him enthusiastically.
4. When he arrives, take the leash near his collar and guide him into a Sit facing you. Do not pull him to you. If he is not coming in correctly, move straight backward as you guide him to a Sit in front of you.
5. Before you do the Finish, take just enough leash—about three feet—to make sure you do not pull on him when giving the command. Yes, your leash is stuck around his legs and yours. Don't worry about it.
6. Do your Finish. Miraculously, the leash is no longer wrapped around Scruffy's legs. It may, however, still be wrapped around yours. Step over it so that it is in front of you.
7. Go forward in the Heel. As you do so, collect the leash.

If, at any time, Scruffy takes a "side trip" during the Recall, pick up your leash and give a sharp tug as you say, "No!" Then drop the leash and allow Scruffy to perform properly while you praise him enthusiastically.

Dogs often become lazy due to lack of incentive. For example, perhaps you weren't praising him enthusiastically as he responded, or the distractions are just too difficult to deal with. Bring out the bait. A small piece of freeze-dried liver or hot dog can be just the thing to put life back into the Recall response.

When using food or a toy reward, do not show Scruffy the incentive before leaving him on a Stay. He won't want to remain there. Instead, show it to him as he begins to come. Keep the bait out in front of you holding it a little below waist height. As Scruffy arrives, lure him into a Sit right in front of your toes, just as you would do for a puppy learning the Come exercise. After he sits, give him his reward. Continue to use the bait for several training sessions, then begin to phase it out by offering it every other time and then every two times. If Scruffy begins to tune you out again, return to using the bait more often.

Sometimes a dog will perform his Come but not come in straight or sit directly in front of his handler. Bait can also remedy this situation. It will draw the dog in straighter and provide a cleaner, faster response. Keep in mind, however, that once started, it must be phased out.

Practice these exercises from both sit and down stays. Call Scruffy from his break time and from different locations around him. Your dog must learn to come directly to you regardless of activity or location. When he is reliable, try doing these exercises while out of sight. Remember, Scruffy won't see that you are not actually holding that leash. After all, the end of it is out of his sight just as you are. He's been Faked Out.

Chapter 14

Changing
of the Guard

Now that we've sufficiently bluffed Scruffy into thinking he's on a leash when he actually isn't, it's time to reduce the use of a training device altogether. This is also done with a Fake Out. The head halter remains on, but you don't really use it—except for emergencies.

Before starting this phase, be sure Scruffy is very reliable on his Stays and Comes. He should very rarely, if ever, break a Stay and be coming directly to you from whatever direction you call him. Essentially, you should be at the point where you don't ever have to correct him on these exercises.

The first part of phasing out a training device is to do so on exercises in which your dog works well, namely, the Stays and Comes. Heeling is one of the last things we'll be doing off-leash because this has far more variables than the Stays and Recalls. With the Stays, Scruffy either remains in place or doesn't. If he doesn't, you return him to the same spot and reiterate your Stay command. On the Recall command, Scruffy either comes or doesn't. Once again, simply back up the command by making him come. However, since Scruffy has advanced this far in his training, your voice alone should be sufficient to replace him into position or guide him to come, so use your vocal control **before** any physical reprimand.

1. Work with Scruffy for at least five minutes, practicing all of the exercises you have learned to this point.
2. Stop and have Scruffy sit in Heel position.
3. Take your long leash off of his head halter and attach it to his regular neck collar.

When reducing the use of the head halter, begin by putting the long leash on the neck collar.

4. Tell your dog to Stay.

5. Gradually increase your distance as you walk around him.

   If, at any point, Scruffy gets up, use your verbal reprimand immediately and quickly move straight toward him. Most likely, Scruffy will seat himself. If not, return him to his spot, tell him to stay and continue to walk around him, gradually increasing your distance.

6. After making at least two complete circles at the end of your long leash, turn and call Scruffy to come.

7. Gather in your lead as he approaches.

8. After he sits before you (and you praise him), switch your leash back to the head halter, give him a reward, and do your Finish.

If Scruffy came in too fast for you to gather your long leash, take hold of the leash within a foot or two of the head halter as he nears you. Have him sit and then switch the leash back to the head halter.

Within a few training sessions you can begin waiting to do this switch after Scruffy performs his Finish. Continue to use your leash in the exact same manner as you had when his leash was attached to his head halter. Scruffy now knows these exercises inside out. He will not need to be guided or corrected at any time—other than with your voice. If he does need more, back up to the previous training stage and continue to work on that for a few more days.

One of the ways to do a proper correction when your long leash is attached to the

Changing of the Guard

The leash is no longer spread out with you on the stays. You leave it near your dog.

This will help in future training sessions when your leash will be attached to the neck collar during all exercises. Once the leash is removed, the only means of doing any physical corrections will be through the pull tab. You can think of it as your insurance. If Scruffy does not listen to your voice, you'll have the pull tab as back-up, proving to your dog that you are still in control.

Now that Scruffy is performing his Stays, you can begin increasing your distance while you walk around him. Do this gradually, and remember, do not move straight out, spiral around. With each stay exercise, increase your distance from him by two feet. Also, continue hiding behind objects for increasing periods of time. Decrease your praise to every so often, instead of constant. Scruffy no longer needs continual voice guidance except when coming to you.

Always return to your leash before calling your dog to come. At this point you should not have to step on the leash anymore.

neck collar is to put a pull tab on the ring of the head halter. This pull tab can be a short leash or a piece of rope knotted and inserted into the ring. Take hold of the tab whenever you need to replace Scruffy into his stay, instead of pulling against his neck collar. Pulling on the neck collar will be fruitless. It is not a training device and will, in turn, cause Scruffy to pull back against it. The last thing you want to do is return to square one and pull on your dog.

The pull tab should remain on Scruffy's head halter at all times.

Guide your dog back to you while you walk backwards. Once he is in front of you, have him stop and sit.

Maintain your dog's attentiveness and motivation by using bait now and then.

Whenever your dog does not stop in proper Heel position, do a Finish.

Do, however, remain close enough to grab it should Scruffy get a bee in his bonnet and decide that yonder stick is too good to pass up.

If, at any time, Scruffy does go after yonder stick, pick up your leash and take a big step backward as you say, "No." This will give his neck collar a little tug. Although this is not really an effective physical reprimand, it does act as a reminder of his mission. When he returns his attention to you, offer enthusias-

tic praise for his proper response. Often the promise of a reward upon arrival is enough incentive to avoid enticing sticks and other distractions.

Should Scruffy overshoot on his come, meaning that he continues beyond his target of sitting in front of you, take hold of the pull tab as he passes, walk straight backward a few steps, and guide him into his proper position. Always praise him as he sits before you, regardless of how he got there.

One way to keep Scruffy from going beyond you is to stand with your back against a solid wall or fence. He'll have no reason to go beyond you. After several repetitions, Scruffy will know that good things happen to dogs that arrive at the correct spot. Namely, praise and rewards.

Every once in a while, even the best trained dogs will test their limits. The last thing you want at this point is for Scruffy to say, "Aha, my person has no control over me when the leash isn't on my head halter." Should this happen, off-lead training will take much longer. You'll have to return to your on-lead work and reassert your Alpha position.

Dogs have their good days and bad days. While you don't want Scruffy to rely on food rewards for executing his commands, you'll occasionally need it to divert his attention from a minor distraction. Also, it'll make most training days good, by offering a little motivation.

Some dogs will come to you very fast when being called from a distance. The further away, the faster the speed. Be prepared for your legs to receive a nose-bruising bump. It's tough to put on the brakes when going ninety miles an hour. You might be able to avoid this crash by telling Scruffy to sit when he's about six to ten feet from you. By the time the command sinks in, he'll have slowed down a bit and started his descent. With the landing gear lowered, he'll place himself before your feet, ears still flapping with the breeze and a grin plastered on his face.

Always offer plenty of praise for a job well done.

Chapter 15

Find Me

Remember the Round Robin game you played when Scruffy was a puppy? We get to play it again, only you'll be using longer distances and going out of sight. Scruffy also now knows much more about listening on command and ignoring distractions, so you'll have a higher degree of reliability while outdoors.

We'll also begin increasing our distance from the leash. You no longer need to back up your commands with it because Scruffy should be very reliable. However, it's a good idea for him to keep wearing it—just in case. This is especially important if you are working him in an unfamiliar setting, a park, or close to a high-traffic area, which in some places is difficult to avoid. He may be reliable enough not to need it, but having it on will make you feel more secure, thereby making him feel the same because he senses your every emotion.

When working on this next level of off-lead training, you can simply drop the leash after telling Scruffy to stay. Continue gradually to increase your distances by spiraling out from him. The main difference will be that you will be calling him without being on a direct line with the leash. This represents a further reduction of your reliance on it.

By now you should be doing your stays and comes from great distances and out of sight. Scruffy will have a wonderful time running from place to place. You can be sure he'll sleep well after one of these training sessions!

Now we begin working on the Heel exercise by reducing physical contact. Attach the long leash to his regular tag-bearing neck collar. Hold the very end of it in your right hand with the rest of it behind your back. Begin heeling by loosely holding the pull tab. The long leash will drag behind. When Scruffy is heeling properly, drop the pull tab. Be sure not to change anything, such as looking back at him. Keep in mind that Scruffy is maintaining pace by remaining

We are now working on having Scruffy listen without direct leash contact.
Do the recall away from the line of the leash.

fixed on your left side. Should your left shoulder fall back as you watch him, he'll naturally slow down.

As you did with the recall command, you'll be using your voice as a guidance system to ensure that Scruffy remains in the appropriate location. Each time he strays even an inch from your side, you'll say, "No," give the pull tab a tug, then drop it again. When he returns to the proper position, praise him.

Be sure never to let Scruffy get so far away that you have to reach for him or step toward him to retrieve the pull tab. Some dogs will think this a game and take off, thereby ruining the entire exercise. Be quick and firm.

Some dogs will tend to lag from the weight of the long leash dragging behind them. Should Scruffy fall behind, try slapping your leg and offering words of encouragement. You are far better off encouraging Scruffy to keep up with you than dragging him forward and intimidating him. Remember, we want this to be fun for him, not a chore and definitely not something of which he'll be fearful. Another means of helping him catch up is to jog forward a few steps. Dogs love running after people. As soon as Scruffy catches up, praise him and return to a brisk walk.

While you work on perfecting this disconnected heeling, do many turns and stops. Each turn will reinforce Scruffy's attention without your having to grab the pull tab. Stopping will also keep his attention on you. The more often you turn and stop, the more attentive Scruffy will remain throughout the training session.

Put the end of the long leash in your right hand so your dog does not have to drag the full weight of the long leash.

Take hold of the pull tab as you begin heeling.

Part of maintaining Scruffy's attention throughout this heeling exercise is knowing which turn to make and when to time your stops. The distance he roams from a proper heeling position will bear on your decisions. If he remains just a little ahead of your left leg, do a sharp left turn. This will immediately put him back in the correct position with the added benefit that he watches you more closely. A right turn should be executed when Scruffy turns to look at something or forges far ahead. You should preferably do the turn while he's looking at the distraction and **before** he forges. However, many of us just aren't that fast, so instead, put your foot on the long leash, say, "No!" and do your right turn. Scruffy will feel the tug on his collar, reminding him of where he's supposed to be. He will then turn around and catch up. As soon as he does, be sure to praise him.

Time your stops for a few steps after you do a turn. It'll be easiest after a left turn. Scruffy will be in position and will likely stop properly. He will be more likely to overshoot after a right turn. When he does so, say "No!" which will make him look back at you. Have him do his finish. After the finish he'll be back in the proper position and should be praised.

As you can see, attaining a proper Heel off-lead depends mostly on your timing and use of appropriate vocal tones. Each tone needs to be very different, and you need to use them quickly and in the proper context. You don't want to be reprimanding Scruffy while he's correcting himself and, likewise, you don't want to be praising him while he's moving ahead of you.

Now we need to put all of these exercises together and make sure we don't get completely entangled in the long leash. Yes, there is a way to be efficient with this!

Let's start with the heeling exercises. You walk around doing turns and stops and decide it's time for a stay. Drop your long leash, tell Scruffy to stay, and move out to whatever distance you have comfortably attained.

Call Scruffy to come. He comes and sits before you, tail wagging and panting with happiness. After a quick pat on the head, do the finish. Unless Scruffy requires a reminder, do not pick up the leash at any time during these exercises.

Now Scruffy is sitting back at your side in heel position. The long leash lies not only around your ankles, but also in a line before you. Take hold of Scruffy's pull tab, tell him to

heel, and step forward toward the end of your long leash. As you near the end loop, pick it up without missing a stride. Now it is dragging behind you. Drop the pull tab and work on your Heel exercise again. See? You never had to disentangle yourself or your dog throughout the entire process!

After working on these exercises for up to two weeks, you and Scruffy should be ready to approach the Final Frontier.

When your dog is attentive you can drop the pull tab.

Chapter 16

The Final Frontier

These are the voyages of the leashless, head halterless dog. He wears only a pull tab and regular neck collar. He responds to verbal and visual cues. When his handler turns, he turns. When his handler leaves, he stays. When his handler calls, he comes—regardless of distraction. Ah, the ideal dog!

The time has come to drop all training devices. Scruffy responds to your voice and body language. He knows many words in your vocabulary and is on his way to doing anything you wish. Whether you're heading to the obedience ring, seeking agility, or just want a pet to go hiking with, Scruffy will be a joy in any situation.

The main difference at this point will be that you take off the long leash. Scruffy will be saying, "Phew, no more weight to drag around," and he'll be less likely to lag.

You may be tempted to work with the long distances again, but don't rush things. Go back to short distance work on your stays and comes. You don't have that long leash for emergencies any more and, should that yonder stick look inviting again, you need to be close enough to Scruffy to take hold of him.

Begin doing your Stays and Comes at six feet. Each time Scruffy performs well, increase the distance by two to five feet. Within one to two training sessions you'll be back at working the long distances and out of sight. However, be cautious and do the distance work in a large, fenced-in area, such as a baseball field. The last thing you need is Scruffy seeing another dog across a busy street and deciding he can't resist her charms.

Once Scruffy is totally reliable on his exercises, it's time to remove the head halter. (This can be anywhere from two to six months from the start of your training.) Attach your pull tab to his regular tag-bearing neck collar. You'll still need a little insurance from time to time, especially if Scruffy

This dog has completed on- and off-lead training. A young dog may still have to wear the halter as reinforcement for an additional two months.

thinks, "Oh boy, no head halter. That means I'm free." Many dogs associate their training devices with behaving. You'll need to make sure Scruffy understands that he must listen even without his head halter.

Keep the pull tab on his collar at all times when you are with him. Every dog challenges their person's authority from time to time, so you need the means of backing up your command without grabbing Scruffy's neck collar.

Begin again with the short distance work. Gradually increase the distances as Scruffy proves reliable. Because this is still very new, return to working with the head halter whenever you are going into a distraction

Should your dog forge ahead of you while heeling, stop and do a Finish.

Always maintain your criteria by making sure Scruffy does a straight Come and Sit.

This is the ideal response when working off-lead.

situation. For example, Scruffy has been performing perfectly in your backyard and even down the road at the park, so you decide to go for a hike in the state forest. There are bound to be other people there with the same idea. There will be children and dogs running around, many of them not under control. Not only that, but there will also be the odors and droppings of wild animals, the enticing sight of woods to run through and streams to swim in. This is a situation in which to return to the use of the head halter because Scruffy will have to learn to resist these new distractions.

As Scruffy proves reliable in new situations, you can gradually reduce the need for the head halter and be confident that he will listen regardless of what he's wearing. And remember, your emotions transfer to him. Should you feel relaxed with the situation, he will too.

You've done it! Scruffy is completely obedience trained. No more training devices! Where do you go from here? Anywhere. You'll need to continue stimulating your dog throughout his life. Keep teaching him new things and taking him to new places. Become involved in dog-related activities with your best friend. It's a great opportunity to meet other people with the same interests. Not only will Scruffy enjoy the socializing, you will too.

Chapter 17

This Is My House

Most dogs have some behavioral problems. There is no escaping it. Dogs are individuals with likes, dislikes, and emotion-driven behavior. They respond to their environment in different ways. Some strive to dominate, others accept, and some even develop anxiety.

The best means of making sure Scruffy doesn't chew the house apart is to teach him as a young pup, but one does not always have this luxury since many pets are acquired while juveniles or adults. Older dogs can turn out to be great companions, but do arrive with behavioral baggage, which is usually why they were homeless in the first place.

Behavior modification goes hand in paw with obedience training. You cannot successfully do one without the other. Opening up the lines of communication between you and your dog through obedience training allows you to teach Scruffy that the house is yours, not his. This includes all socks, shoes, towels, carpets, couches, and anything on counters and tables. You'll deal with the delivery person, and you will have guests from time to time and expect them to be treated with the utmost respect and courtesy. Scruffy will have his own toys and bed. You have yours. Scruffy is not to make what is yours into his. Moreover, you intend to walk out the door without paw prints all over your clothing.

While you may feel that you are bombarding Scruffy with too much at one time by teaching him to behave and to listen to commands, you have no other choice. To allow an infraction is to set a precedent. Whatever bad behavior you allow upon his arrival will be harder to correct later.

Most dogs need to learn their limitations quickly. In fact, they like learning the house rules so that they can discern their place in the family pack. They then relax, knowing someone else is in charge. Being a leader has many responsibilities that can make a dog hyper, aggressive, and pushy. These "leader dogs" are rarely happy, relaxed dogs.

Jumping Up

The most widespread complaint with one's pet is that they jump up. Even some very well-trained dogs jump up. The rule should be that Scruffy can only jump up if invited or may not do so at all. Generally, you should begin with the "not at all" rule. It'll be easier for Scruffy to understand; dogs believe in a strict difference between may and may not. They don't have "sometimes" in their language, and they don't understand "maybe," or "it's okay this time but not next time."

Before teaching Scruffy to not jump up, you should understand why he's doing it in the first place. The jump up is for one of two reasons. First, he may have learned that when he jumps on you, he receives attention. Second, dogs greet each other by putting their noses close together, then going around the back and taking a sniff. Scruffy may simply want to give you the appropriate greeting, and you're making it difficult with your nose so high in the air.

Begin overcoming the jumping by first solving the reasons for it. With the attention issue, simply don't give it. Walk away. Or, better yet, step back quickly before Scruffy gets his paws up on you. He'll discover that he's wasting all that energy and may stop jumping. Teaching him to sit for attention will be a more positive means of offering him the reward of a pat on the head or a tummy rub. You should always make your dog do something to receive his rewards. Giving a reward for doing nothing will earn you a pushy dog.

Unless you're afraid of being bowled over by a large, enthusiastic dog, crouch down to Scruffy's level to allow for a proper greeting. Over the time you spend working on obedience, Scruffy will learn that he needs to contain himself better in order for you to say hello.

Curing an existing problem of a large dog jumping all over you can be done in a few seconds, **without** stepping on his toes, squeezing his front paws, or kneeing him in the chest. There is never any need to hurt your dog when you train him. Keep in mind that punching, yelling, and holding a grudge are not in the canine language. Using these tactics will only frustrate Scruffy and possibly make him aggressive.

If you have his head halter on, you can pull forward and upward on it when Scruffy tries to jump up or, if he has already done so, first tug down to get him down and then the forward and up motion to make him sit.

Another means of curing this, when you don't have the luxury of a head halter on, is to make a No Jump box. This consists of a small metal can with approximately fifteen pennies inside. A tea tin, metal Band-Aid box, or small coffee can would work well. Do not use aluminum. It does not make the proper sound, and some dogs will think you're offering another toy. You should make several No Jump boxes and place them in all the locations where Scruffy is likely to jump—the doors, kitchen, family room, and one for the road.

When Scruffy starts to jump, you'll see his haunches bunch up, and he'll be looking upward. Try to use your verbal reprimand at this point so that you correct him for even thinking about it. If this doesn't work, shake the can hard in an up-and-down motion once or twice. Scruffy will move away and stare at you. Tell him to sit. When he does so, praise and pet him. Use this technique each time he jumps, and you will see a quick decrease in the behavior. He simply won't do it anymore. Not only is this very effective, it is also a very fast cure. That's not to say he won't still try from time to time, especially on children or visitors. You can be assured that your guest will not correct Scruffy for his behavior. Some might even say that it's okay for him to jump on them. Maybe so, but it's not okay with you, and therefore Scruffy should never do it—the all-or-nothing law in effect. No Jump boxes should be strategically placed throughout your house for emergency use. If Scruffy greets someone at the door by jumping up, you shake the can. Should Scruffy get overexuberant with a child and jump up, shake the can.

This brings up the next subjects: getting into the garbage and jumping on countertops. The No Jump box will be useful for these bad habits as well. There's only one drawback. It generally only works if you're there to shake the can. Many dogs, however, do associate the ugly can sound with the No Jump box itself. Placing the box near the garbage can or on the counter often has the same effect as putting a fence around those things. Scruffy will make a wide berth when he sees the can.

Many dogs, though, will not respect the sight of the No Jump box without the sound. These dogs will need special handling to teach them to not rummage on the counters and in the garbage. Sure, they learn to respect these things while you're around, but go into the family room and visit with guests while leaving the Thanksgiving turkey on the counter, and you'll find that the only one enjoying the holiday meal will be Scruffy.

One means of making sure you get your dinner is to place all food way out of reach, which can be difficult if you own an Irish Wolfhound or Great Dane. Their reach is farther than that of most humans.

The same for the garbage. You can put it in a cabinet to avoid having to clean it up from all over the house after Scruffy has had his fun. The only problem with this is that you have rearranged your life, and your dog hasn't learned anything.

If you want to confront these problems and teach Scruffy that his food only comes in his dish, you will need to do the following:

1. Put the long leash on Scruffy's head halter.

This dog is learning not to jump on the counter. Bait is placed within reach. The dog is wearing his head halter and twenty-foot lead so that he can be properly corrected if he jumps up.

A Buster Cube is a great means of keeping Scruffy busy for a while.

2. Place something enticing on the edge of the counter or trash can. Make sure Scruffy sees you place it.

3. Hang on to the end of the leash and go around the corner.

4. Peek into the kitchen and watch.

5. As soon as Scruffy sniffs at the bait, use your verbal reprimand and give a hefty yank on the leash.

6. Return to the kitchen and make Scruffy do a long Down/Stay, then praise him and give him a reward, such as a pat on the head.

7. Repeat as often as necessary until Scruffy no longer sniffs the bait.

The next phase involves taking off the head halter and leash. You still need to use the bait and hide around the corner. It may take a while before Scruffy decides to chance it. As soon as he does, use your verbal reprimand, go into the kitchen and put him in a Down/Stay. Again, praise him and pat him after he remains for at least three minutes. You always need to praise your dog for doing something that you request, regardless of a previous bad behavior. You may need to continue this process for a few weeks. Until Scruffy no longer thinks about jumping on the counter or raiding the trash can, make sure he doesn't have access to that area at any time while you are not there. This includes your short trip to the powder room. It only takes three seconds for a dog to snatch something off a counter and take the goody into hiding for future enjoyment.

Another means of curing these problems is to redirect Scruffy's attention onto a positive outlet. Teach Scruffy to go to a special spot and investigate a particular toy whenever you put food on the counter. To do this, take a hollow toy, such as a sterilized bone, Buster Cube, or Kong and put some of his kibble, cheese, or peanut butter inside. Place your food on the counter, and then put the toy in Scruffy's place and teach Scruffy to remain in a Down/Stay and play with his toy the entire time the food remains on the counter. Within a short time Scruffy will learn that food on the counter means treats and fun at his place, and he'll automatically go to his place. As the idea sinks in, begin to offer the toy a little later each time after Scruffy goes to his place. He'll learn to remain at his place with the expectation of receiving his special toy. Always praise him and offer his reward of the special treat-filled toy within a reasonable amount of time—say, two to three minutes. You must continue to associate this special reward with the fact that there's food on the counters, or he'll figure out that the food on the counter is more enticing than waiting for his toy.

Destructive Chewing

Chewing is the second most common complaint of dog owners. Usually, they finally decide to train their dogs after they've lost a couch or pair of designer shoes. By this time their relationship with Scruffy is strained, at best. Keep in mind that the losses could be avoided by training Scruffy as a youngster. However, if you obtained him with this added liability, you can still cure him. If you obtained your dog from the shelter or a rescue organization, chances are ten to one that he has this problem. Destructive chewing is one of the most prevalent reasons that people give up their dogs.

First of all, you need to understand why dogs chew. It can either begin with teething and they weren't properly redirected to appropriate chew toys, or occur latently due to boredom and/or anxiety. You must remember that chewing is how dogs amuse themselves. They don't read books, play baseball, board games, chat on the Internet, and rarely watch television—unless the program involves barking dogs. Chewing is one of their only pastimes when their people don't want to play with them.

Working with a Puppy

Early learning can prevent a rampant chewing problem. Your pup will begin his oral discoveries before his baby teeth start falling out. This is when he will put his jaws on the table legs, chairs, and molding. You need to be there to redirect his attention onto his own chew toys. When you can't watch him he should be contained in an area where he can't get into any trouble.

When you see young Scruffy put his mouth where it shouldn't be, you can use your No Jump box to startle him. If the box isn't handy, use your verbal reprimand and push him away from whatever his teeth are on. Immediately present him with one of his own chew toys and play with him. As he plays with his own toy, praise him.

You must keep a constant watch on a youngster, as they can quickly turn from chewing on their own toy to the nearby wall or chair leg that they are resting against.

Working with an Older Dog

The same procedures can be used successfully on an older dog as well. Keep him confined when you can't be there and watch him like a hawk when you are in the room with him. Should he put his teeth around the chair leg, use the No Jump box or your verbal reprimand. It would also help to keep a head halter on him with a light leash dragging so that you can grab the leash and give it a tug to move his head away from the object he is chewing.

Always make sure Scruffy has a variety of chew toys and that you rotate them to keep him interested. He'll need toys that bounce, toys he can dig his teeth into, and toys that jingle or squeak.

Another way you can avoid damage to your home is to spray a bad-tasting substance on everything that Scruffy likes to chew on. This can include his bed, for many dogs, if left alone for long periods of time, will chew their beds into millions of pieces. Replacing beds can get expensive after a while.

Some breeds, however, such as German Shepherds, actually like the taste of these things. In this case you'll just need to be sure the dog is confined when you aren't around and keep him in the same room with you (use the head halter with the light leash attached) when you are home. He may need to sleep on the hard floor or crate tray for a while until he learns to stop destroying his bed.

Many dogs become destructive due to separation anxiety. This is often seen when Scruffy's person is suddenly away from home for longer than usual. Such behavior is also common in dogs that have had several different owners and homes. They have been abandoned so often that the fear of it happening again makes them extremely anxious.

When a dog develops separation anxiety, he exhibits his distress by chewing objects that carry his person's scent. This is usually the carpeting by the door, but also includes shoes, furniture, and cabinets.

One of the ways to help Scruffy overcome this problem is to give him a playmate, such as another dog. Dogs are social animals and instinctively need to be with their pack. Separated, they develop anxieties and neuroses. Another dog will offer some pack unity while you are away. You may also find that confining Scruffy will help relieve some of his anxiety. Remaining in a denlike area, such as a crate or small room, will make him feel safer than if given the entire house to roam. This also makes sure nothing is destroyed, and Scruffy doesn't end up in the emergency room because of swallowing stockings and other nondigestible items.

Offering Scruffy a special chew toy just before you leave may also help. He'll have something to do while you're gone. Before you know it, he'll be waiting by the door anxiously awaiting his good-bye treat. Don't worry, he'll still be happy to see you when you come home. He just won't be so upset anymore when you leave because he has good associations with the event.

Should Scruffy have severe separation anxiety, your veterinarian can prescribe a tranquilizer, such as Clomicalm, to help him adjust. The Clomicalm Plan combined with simple behavioral guidelines will help eliminate the problem. Scruffy will eventually understand that nothing bad will happen while he is alone.

Excessive Indoor Barking

Another common behavior problem is excessive barking. This is more prevalent in smaller breeds, such as Shelties, Terriers, and Toy Poodles, but any breed in which the individual feels the need to be the Alpha figure could become an excessive barker. They bark at the delivery people, neighbors walking down the street, dogs on their territory, and often when they hear another dog barking up to a mile away. You didn't hear the bark, but Scruffy sure did, and he's going to let you know about it.

The Alpha dog must always strive to protect his territory and won't listen to the Beta and Omega people who tell him to be quiet, because they don't know how to perform the job properly. If his people had, then they'd relieve him of his duties.

The first means of curing this problem is to go through obedience training. This will teach Master Scruffy that he is not the boss. He must listen to what his people tell him to do, and if one of those commands is to shut his yap, so be it. He no longer needs to guard the house because he has learned that his people will take care of the job just fine.

Next, you'll need to distract Scruffy whenever he feels the need to sound off. As he rushes to the door at the sound of the door bell, bring him away from the door and place him in a Down/Stay. You may need someone to help you at first; you can't back up the command while answering the door, because as soon as you leave to see who's at the door, Scruffy is on your heels and gets there first. You need to remain at his side and each time he pops up, he must be replaced in his Down/Stay by first pulling forward and up to make him sit, and then downward as

you put pressure on his shoulder blades until his belly touches the floor. No matter how many times you must replace him, continue to do so. You must follow through with your command or not bother giving it at all.

Should Scruffy continue barking, even though he has been placed in a submissive position (the Down/Stay), take hold of his muzzle, look him in the eye and say, "NO BARK!" or another word that you might prefer, in a low tone of voice. Maintain your hold on his muzzle until he looks away from you. Each time he barks, do the same correction. Essentially, you are telling him that you are the boss, and he is not to sound off.

Put one hand on the collar to keep your dog steady and wrap your other hand around his muzzle. Look directly into his eyes and say, "NO BARK!" in a low tone of voice. Maintain the hold until he looks away from you.

The head halter is also helpful in performing this correction. You can pull upward under Scruffy's chin, which closes his mouth. He can't bark effectively with his mouth closed. This is the same correction as when you took Scruffy's muzzle and held it shut while you used your verbal reprimand, only easier. Unlike holding his muzzle, Scruffy can't get away from you when you use the head halter.

Everyone wants a dog that will bark to let them know when someone is at the door or in their yard. It doesn't matter if you have a small or large dog. It's just nice to know when someone has arrived. For this reason you don't want to teach Scruffy to never bark, only to turn off the loudspeaker on command.

This can be done the same way as with the previous situation. First, however, you want to praise Scruffy for letting you know someone is there, and then give him the "Quiet" or "No Bark" command as well as a Sit or Down/Stay. You don't want to be hanging onto your dog as you answer the door. You and Scruffy are much more efficient if he is totally under control.

Begin by making sure Scruffy is wearing his head halter and light leash. Heel with him to the door and make sure he sits at your side. Any more sounding off is corrected with the muzzle hold and Alpha stare, or if he can successfully keep dodging your hand as you grab for his muzzle, use the head halter. Pull upward on the head halter. This both shuts his mouth so he can't bark and replaces him into the Sit/Stay—all with one hand.

Continue to hold the leash, loosely, as you answer the door. Each time Scruffy pops up, replace him. He needs to learn to do Sit/Stays at the door anyway, because the last thing you need is for him to squeeze through your legs and go running out into the street.

These tactics can also be used while you and Scruffy are out and about, and he sees another dog that he must bark at. Simply pull forward on the head halter until he settles down and then continue with your training session. Never get nervous or anxious, for this is quickly communicated to Scruffy through your actions and scent. Remain calm and purposeful, and your dog will learn to do the same. Scruffy will then decide if the Alpha (you) doesn't respond to that strange animal or person, he should not respond either. After all, you are the leader and, if you remain calm and comfortable with a situation, he should follow suit.

Digging and Outdoor Barking

Often one has to deal with a dog who might be an angel indoors but a monster outdoors. If you intend to keep Scruffy outside, don't expect to maintain your landscaping. He'll dig up the grass simply by running around and when the weather gets hot, he'll dig holes under plants to find a cool place to rest.

If you want to maintain some sort of yard, you will have to watch Scruffy while he plays in it. Begin by taking him out with his head halter and long leash. Allow him to run around and relieve himself. However, if he begins digging, give the long lead a hard tug and use your verbal reprimand. Don't wait until he's dug down a few inches. Correct him the second you see those paws at work. The same goes for chewing plants. When his mouth goes around that azalea give a hard tug and verbal reprimand.

Going out with Scruffy and guiding him in this manner will teach him the laws of the yard. It's your yard. He is not to do anything without your consent. Do your obedience training in the yard to let him know that he is to listen wherever he may be, even where he plays.

Correcting Scruffy will be much more difficult when he is outside and you are inside or not home. Should he be an excessive barker, don't leave him outside when you are away from home. Otherwise, the only means of stopping him is to have him wear a barker breaker collar. These come in many different varieties from one that sprays citronella, to a distracting tone, to an electrical stimulation. Always begin with the least offensive type first. It may be enough. Try to avoid having to use the type with electrical stimulation. While the zap doesn't cause any short- or long-term damage and does stop the barking quickly, you are better off trying to correct the problem in a positive manner instead of using negative reinforcement.

If you leave Scruffy indoors and receive reports from neighbors that he constantly barks, try conditioning him as follows:

1. Pretend to leave for work. Do everything that you would normally do before you leave. This includes taking the car keys. If Scruffy has a view of the driveway, get in your car and drive down the block. Park your car and sneak back to your house.
2. The second Scruffy barks, quickly go inside and correct him in the manner previously described.
3. Go out again.
4. Should Scruffy go back to barking, again return and correct him.
5. Try remaining outside for five minutes. If Scruffy is silent, return and praise him. He should even get a treat. Make a fuss over him to teach him that being quiet has its rewards.
6. Gradually increase the amount of time before returning and praising.

This is the most positive means of correcting an indoor dog from excessive barking. You can try it with a dog that remains outside, but it's more difficult to hide from him. He may be able to both see and smell you. If nothing else, he will most definitely smell you unless you are a good distance away, and this would make your returning and correcting him difficult, especially if he automatically stopped barking as soon as he knew you were there. You can't correct him when he isn't doing it.

Sometimes, offering a special chew toy just before leaving will work as well on the barking of a lonely dog as it does on the antics of a dog with separation anxiety. Scruffy will be keeping his mouth busy with the toy instead of with sounding off. It's tough to do both at the same time. This will also maintain his effectiveness as a burglar deterrent, for he'll only stop chewing when he hears an intruder and return to chewing when the intruder is gone. You hope.

Dogs and Cats

Those with both cats and dogs will sometimes have to deal with Scruffy chasing Muffy through the house. Granted, Muffy had probably teased Scruffy into the chase, but there should nevertheless be some control over the situation. This behavior is most often seen with juvenile puppies or dogs that were not raised with cats. You must teach your dog to not chase, or Muffy will end up hurt or worse. Of course, Scruffy could also end up with the raw end of the deal: scratches across his nose.

When you are away from home make sure that the cat and dog have no means of being in the same place at the same time. One or both will need to be confined.

When you are home, make sure Scruffy is wearing his head halter with the leash attached. When you see the cat approach, take a light hold of the leash. Don't do anything until Scruffy reacts. Muffy will slink under his nose and flick her tail in his face. At that point he simply can't resist. All four paws are running in place, ready for take off. Muffy sees her chance to begin the chase and makes a run for the next room. Immediately use your verbal reprimand and give a firm tug on the leash. Give Scruffy a Down/Stay command and make him maintain it for a few minutes. This will take his mind off of that teasing cat and onto something more constructive.

You'll need to continue using this technique should Muffy decide to jump on a chair and further tease Scruffy by waving her paws at him and hissing. No dog can resist that torment.

Scruffy must learn to ignore Muffy, and this is best done by putting him to work. In fact, keeping Scruffy under one command or another maintains your control over him and gives him something to do. Dogs enjoy performing for their people. The chance to work for hours on end, even if it is only the simple

This child, who is fearful of dogs, is more confident when the dog is introduced to him in a Down/Stay.

Sit and Down/Stay, will make Scruffy relaxed and happy.

Then again, it wouldn't be a bad idea to teach Muffy a thing or two. It's not fair that Scruffy has to be the only one that must maintain control. Yes, cats can be trained! In fact, they enjoy learning to come, sit, stay, lie down, and jump from one place to another. Many even learn to heel. All it takes is fifteen minutes of your time each day and an irresistible feline treat. You can approach cat training the exact same way you taught Scruffy puppy kindergarten, only without the head halter and substituting the freeze-dried liver with tuna fish.

Children and Dogs

Often dogs will become excited when they see children. To a dog, a child is like a puppy—someone to play with. The danger is that dogs play a lot rougher than a child can withstand. Scruffy needs to learn to be sedate and careful around both children and the elderly.

When you have this problem, you had best keep the head halter on Scruffy with the light leash attached. Upon greeting a child or an elderly person, put Scruffy in a Down/Stay. This position will be less threatening to a child, especially if Scruffy is a large breed.

Keep Scruffy in this position while the child says hello. In fact, throughout the time the child or elderly person is around, keep Scruffy under command. When you move around, have him heel at your side. When you stop, he should sit. When you want to move elsewhere and don't want him directly next to you, place him in a stay. Should he be in the same room with these visitors, keep him in a Down/Stay.

When Scruffy has learned proper behavior and does not become overenthusiastic, you can release him from work and allow him to socialize. Always remain alert; he might get excited from time to time. Should he start to jump around or get pushy, put him back in the Down/Stay.

It often helps to teach the child how to give Scruffy commands. Not only will the child feel great power over the dog, but Scruffy will learn to be more respectful of the child.

About Aggression

To learn how to deal with and eliminate aggression you must first understand the different types and how they came about. Some are more dangerous than others, and many can be controlled or virtually eliminated with consistent head halter training.

Most aggressive dogs have become so because of improper socialization and/or lack of proper training. However, never try to cure an aggressive dog through using what you read in a book. Always obtain the help of a professional behaviorist or trainer.

As with all behavior problems, the best means of eliminating them is through prevention. To avert aggressive tendencies, begin with early socialization. Expose your puppy to other dogs and people, especially children. Train your puppy early and never chain him up or isolate him in any manner for long periods of time. Teach your pup that whatever he has in his possession, whether it is a toy, food, or something he is not supposed to have, he must easily give it up to you and all family members, including the children. Never allow him to run the fence and bark at neighbors. And as much as you want to cuddle with him on your lap or bed, make sure he knows his place in your pack is not equal to yours.

Regardless of the type of aggression, dogs don't bite without reason. Bites are always provoked in some way, shape, or form. Most of us just don't realize how we provoked the bite. Always look back on an incident and analyze it as objectively as possible.

There are many types of aggression. A few are as follows.

Defensive or **fear aggression** is associated with fear or pain. You can recognize a fear aggressive dog by his stance. He'll often back away or hide while growling and showing his teeth. He will hold his body low to the ground, tail between his legs, stretch his neck, and raise the fur along his spine. Some fear aggressive dogs will bite as you move away from them, thereby nipping the back of the heel or leg.

A fear aggressive dog must be worked with gently and slowly. You never want him to feel he has no way out. The head halter works very well in this situation. As soon as it is on you'll see a difference in Scruffy's behavior. Through obedience training you can gradually desensitize him from his fears. He'll learn to understand you and his environment, making daily life less stressful. It would be a good idea to utilize a lot of coaxing and bait to help this dog progress. Should he not appear interested in the bait, crouch down a lot, slap your leg, and speak in soothing tones. It may take a few minutes, but the dog will soon respond because he wants to be part of the pack.

Maternal aggression is used to protect. This is most often seen when a mother dog is near her young puppies. Provided she is properly socialized, a mother dog is more likely to show aggression toward another dog than to her people. There is no need to utilize head halters in this situation unless you absolutely cannot avoid having another dog near the mother and her brood.

Dominance aggression is used to maintain control and position in the pack. A dog with this personality tries to make himself look as large as possible. He walks high on his toes, hackles raised, tail up stiff and wagging slowly. His ears are forward and eyes staring. A dominant dog may also put his front paws on the back of another while he growls. These dogs will often mount others and/or bite at their necks.

The head halter is the best tool for teaching a dominant aggressive dog that you are in charge of him. By controlling his head and thus the rest of his body you do not allow him to position himself into an aggressive stance. Should he growl at you, you can pull forward and up on the leash, closing his mouth, as you stare him in the eyes. Keep him in that position until he looks away from you. With the head halter on you can avoid being bitten or jumped on. The dog will have no choice but to sit and listen.

Territorial aggression is similar to dominance aggression, but a dog uses it more to protect territory than to assert position. A territorially aggressive dog will growl, bark, and challenge when someone is either about to enter or already has entered what the dog deems his territory. Territorial aggression can also be considered possessive aggression. This occurs when you try to take away a favorite toy or move the dog from his desired position on the couch.

Territorial aggression can be handled in a manner similar to dominance aggression. The main difference will be that he is not directing his aggression toward you (unless you are taking something away), so there will be no need to hold his nose up in the air until he stops growling. Simply make him sit by pulling forward and upward on the lead. As soon as he sits, release the tension. Each time he opens his mouth to bark at the intruder use your no bark, command and tug upward under his chin.

Predatory aggression is used while hunting and is directed solely at prey.

Learned aggression is the most prevalent in pets. This often occurs when a dog is hit or yelled at. Learned aggression is manifest due to environmental factors. Either the dog has learned that no one is in charge and he must take that position, or that there is no way out of a negative situation and his only recourse is to be aggressive.

The best means of curing this problem is to simply follow the plan of training with a head halter that has been outlined in this book. Through proper training and communication techniques, the learned aggression will be controlled or eliminated.

Disease-induced aggression is caused from the pain or discomfort of an illness. For example, Scruffy has arthritis and he is accidentally touched in a sore area. The best means of dealing with this is to be aware of Scruffy's physical condition and treat him accordingly. Anyone can become grouchy when in pain—ourselves included.

Idiopathic aggression occurs spontaneously, seemingly without reason, although if the dog is to receive a full examination, a dysfunction or genetic basis can often be found as the causative factor.

All types of aggression have a genetic base. Whether the dog is biting out of fear or dominance, there is something in the dog's genetic make-up that makes it prone to such behaviors.

Each type of aggression needs to be handled in an appropriate manner. One must first diagnose before addressing how to eliminate the behavior.

The best way of knowing which type you're dealing with, and it's very important to understand this before starting any training, is to get some information about Scruffy's parents and siblings. Should your dog be a purebred, you shouldn't have too much difficulty procuring the information. If you know the breeder, call and talk with him/her. Registration papers often list the

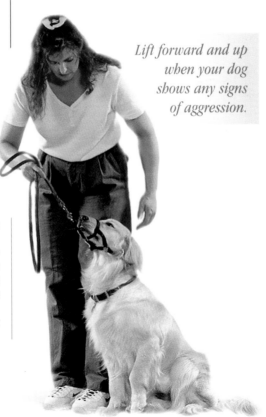

Lift forward and up when your dog shows any signs of aggression.

names and registration numbers of the breeders. You can contact the American Kennel Club for phone numbers. Scruffy's breeder may give you the names and phone numbers of the owners of Scruffy's siblings. The owners of Scruffy's siblings will be able to tell you whether or not their dogs have exhibited the same behavioral tendencies. Any responsible breeder will not have a problem giving out this information because they don't want to ruin the breed by bringing aggressive dogs into the world. A responsible breeder strives to improve a dog breed.

What if Scruffy came from a shelter or rescue group? Then you have no means of finding out about his past. Many dogs, even overtly aggressive ones, may not show their true colors when not on their own territory, so you may never know. However, you can ask the personnel of the facilities if they saw any aggressive behavior while he was there. There is a chance that someone had noticed something.

The head halter plays an important role in eliminating almost any type of aggression. It's a means in which you can safely correct Scruffy without either hurting him or yourself.

Should Scruffy show aggressive tendencies, he must wear the head halter at all times when he is with you or a member of your family. Attach a regular four to six foot leash to his halter and let him drag it around. Unless Scruffy is a small dog, you don't want to use a light leash, for the strain of a confrontation might snap it. He may step on the leash from time to time, but that is far better than not having any control over his outbursts.

Each time he so much as challenges with a direct stare, pull upward under his chin and hold him there for up to ten seconds or until the growling stops. Once

released, make him do a Down/Stay. Should he resist, take the leash in your right hand and pull downward as you put lots of pressure on his shoulder blades. Your pull on the head halter will prevent him from biting you. As soon as he is down, tell him to stay. Each time he pops up, replace him in the down/stay. Remember that the down is a submissive position. When you do this procedure you are simulating what the Alpha dog might do had this scenario been played out in the wild. The Alpha dog would first grab the upstart around the neck or facial area and growl, maintaining hold until the offending dog lay down and/or showed submission.

The person Scruffy challenges should be the person to correct him. A young child should not try this, however, because most dogs have more strength and stamina than a child. To prevent Scruffy from hurting a child, keep him with you at all times and under a command, such as Down/Stay, whenever the child is present.

Unfortunately, sad as it may seem, Scruffy may never be 100 percent reliable and may possibly hurt your child at some point. There are many instances in which this can happen. Scruffy takes food from the youngster's hand, and in his fervor nicks a finger at the same time. Another situation, which is totally psychological, is the occurrence of displaced aggression. Many dogs, when corrected by the Alpha figure, will turn their aggression on an individual who has not shown the dog that they are also Alpha. This is common in wild dog packs, as the pecking order is reestablished after a tussle. Thus, after you correct Scruffy for showing aggression, he in turn reestablishes his Beta (second in command) position by threatening your child, whom he sees as an Omega (lowest in the hierarchy) pack member.

Scruffy must receive daily training sessions, and you should never give in to anything he demands. This goes for something as simple as attention. Should he come to you and either bark at you, put his paw on you, or lean against you, push him away and make him do a down/stay. Pet him on your terms and when you want to. Giving in, even a little bit, will cause everything you're striving for to backfire. Scruffy will see that he does have control over you and his efforts to regain the Alpha position will double.

Also, should there be specific situations in which Scruffy shows aggression, then prevent those situations from occurring. For example, Scruffy growls at you when you try to take him off your furniture. The answer here is simple. Don't allow him on your furniture in the first place. Allowing him to sleep in your bed or rest on your couch has elevated him to equal status and beyond—to Alpha status. Another example in which aggression might occur is when you try to take a toy from him. Many dogs become quite angry if their steak bone is taken away. Essentially, Scruffy is telling you what to do.

Avoid letting Scruffy have that particular type of toy.

Avoiding all things that set off aggression is not **always** a good thing, however. Should Scruffy show aggression when he sees another dog, you must confront the situation by working him in the presence of other dogs. The same goes for joggers or people on bicycles. Confront the situation and work him through it. Any time Scruffy growls, lunges, and barks, pull forward and up on the head halter until he settles into a sit and then immediately put him back to work. He'll quickly learn that he must defer to you—the Alpha of the pack—and that you won't stand for his aggressive behavior in any situation.

Head halters are the saving grace for dogs who are resistant to the use of bait, tend to pull a lot, or show aggressive tendencies. They quickly learn that you are in control. Where the head goes, the body follows. And isn't it nice that you can teach your dog through the use of logic instead of pain?

Go ahead. Get that dog going! You and Scruffy have a great relationship ahead of you.

Appendix

How to Fit a
Head Halter

Halti, Comfort Halter, or K-9 Kumalong

Breed of Dog	Sex of Dog	Halter Size
Sporting Breeds:		
Brittany Spaniel	Female	2
	Male	2–3
English Pointer	Female	2–3
	Male	3–4
German Shorthair Pointer	Female	2–3
	Male	3–4
Chesapeake Bay Retriever	Female	2–3
	Male	3–4
Golden Retriever	Female	3
	Male	3–4
Labrador Retriever	Female	3
	Male	3–4
English Setter/Gordon Setter	Female	3
	Male	3–4

How to Fit a Head Halter

Breed of Dog	Sex of Dog	Halter Size
Irish Setter	Female or Male	3
Cocker Spaniel	Female	1
	Male	2
English Springer Spaniel	Female or Male	2
Vizsla	Female	2–3
	Male	3
Weimaraner	Female	2–3
	Male	3
Hounds:		
Afghan Hound	Female or Male	3
Basset Hound	Female or Male	2–3
Beagle	Female	1–2
	Male	2
Bloodhound	Female	4
	Male	4–5
Borzoi	Female	3
	Male	3–4
Dachshund	Female	0–1
	Male	1
Greyhound	Female	3
	Male	3–4
Norwegian Elkhound	Female or Male	2–3
Rhodesian Ridgeback	Female	3
	Male	3–4
Whippet	Female	2
	Male	2–3
Working Breeds:		
Akita	Female	3
	Male	4
Malamute	Female	3
	Male	4
Boxer	Female	2–3
	Male	3
Doberman Pinscher	Female or Male	3–4
Giant Schnauzer	Female or Male	3–4
Great Dane	Female	4–5
	Male	5
Great Pyrenees	Female	4–5
	Male	5
Jack Russell Terrier	Female	0–1
	Male	1

How to Fit a Head Halter

Breed of Dog	Sex of Dog	Halter Size
Mastiff	Female	4–5
	Male	5
Newfoundland	Female	4–5
	Male	5
Rottweiler	Female	3–4
	Male	4
Saint Bernard	Female	4–5
	Male	5
Samoyed	Female or Male	3–4
Siberian Husky	Female or Male	3
Standard Schnauzer	Female	2–3
	Male	3
Terriers:		
Airedale Terrier	Female or Male	2–3
American Staffordshire	Female	3
	Male	3–4
Border Terrier	Female	1–2
	Male	2
Cairn Terrier	Female or Male	1–2
Miniature Schnauzer	Female	1
	Male	1–2
Scottish Terrier	Female	1–2
	Male	2
Wheaten Terrier	Female or Male	1–2
West Highland White Terrier	Female	1
	Male	1–2
Miscellaneous Breeds:		
Chow Chow	Female or Male	2–3
Dalmatian	Female	2–3
	Male	3
Keeshond	Female or Male	2
Miniature Poodle	Female or Male	1–2
Standard Poodle	Female or Male	2–3
Schipperke	Female or Male	1
Herding Breeds:		
Australian Cattle Dog	Female or Male	2
Bearded Collie	Female or Male	2–3
Belgian Malinois	Female	2–3
	Male	3–4
Bouvier des Flandres	Female	3–4
	Male	4

How to Fit a Head Halter

Breed of Dog	Sex of Dog	Halter Size
Rough Collie (long haired)	Female or Male	3
German Shepherd Dog	Female	3
	Male	3–4
Old English Sheepdog	Female or Male	3
Shetland Sheepdog	Female	1–2
	Male	2
Corgi	Female or Male	1–2
Border Collie	Female or Male	2–3
American Eskimo Dog	Female	1
	Male	1–2
Australian Shepherd	Female	2–3
	Male	3

Measuring according to weight:

Under 20 pounds	Size 0
20–30 pounds	Size 1
30–45 pounds	Size 2
45–60 pounds	Size 3
60–80 pounds	Size 4
Over 80 pounds	Size 5

The Gentle Leader, a figure 8 halter, ranges in size from petite to extra large. They can correspond to the conventional halter sizes as follows:

Petite = Size 0
Small = Size 1
Medium = Size 2–3
Large = Size 4
Extra Large = Size 5

The BeHave and Snoot Loop halters run in only three sizes: Small, Medium, and Large. The Snoot Loop also offers two petite sizes for use on small and toy dogs.

Index

Index

Index